LIFE SKILLS FOR Teens

Practical Strategies to Overcome Self-Doubt & Build Self Confidence - Boost Test Scores and Kick Start Your Game Plan for Extra Money

Skilset Publishing@ Copyright 2023

Date: 11/12/2023

I, the undersigned, hereby declare that I am the sole owner and creator of the work described below, which is being submitted to Skilset Publishing for copyright protection.

Title of Work: Life Skills for Teens: Practical Strategies to Overcome Self Doubt and Build Confidence, Boost Test Scores and Kick Start Your Game Plan for Extra Money

Author: K.R. Heywood

I affirm that I am the exclusive copyright owner of the work mentioned above, and I hereby grant copyright protection to Skilset Publishing.

I grant Skilset Publishing the exclusive rights to reproduce, distribute, display, and publish the work in any form or medium.

This copyright grant is effective from the date of submission and continues for the duration of the copyright protection period.

This copyright grant cannot be revoked except in writing with the mutual agreement of both parties.

I represent and warrant that the work is original, does not infringe upon the rights of any third party, and that I have the legal authority to grant the rights specified herein.

Table of contents

Chapter 1: Building Self-Esteem and Confidence _____ *1*
    Self-Esteem _____ 2
    Understanding Self-Esteem _____ 2
    The Impact of Self-Esteem on Life _____ 3
    Identifying Areas for Improvement _____ 4
    Case Study _____ 5
    Emma's Journey to Boosted Self-Esteem _____ 5
    Personal Anecdote _____ 6
    Self-Compassion _____ 9
    Building a Positive Self-Image _____ 9
    Developing Self-Compassion _____ 9
    Setting and Achieving Goals _____ 10
    Recognizing Self-Doubt Patterns _____ 12
    Overcoming Negative Self-Talk _____ 12
    Seeking Support and Mentorship _____ 13
    Start Today: _____ 14

Chapter 2: Acing your Exams _____ *19*
    Effective Study Techniques _____ 20
    Time management and study schedules. _____ 21
    Active Learning _____ 22
    Mindful Studying _____ 23
        Techniques to Enhance Focus _____ 24
    Avoiding Procrastination _____ 27
    Dealing with Exam Anxiety _____ 28
    Strategies for Managing Stress _____ 28
    Test Preparation and Organization _____ 29
    Seeking Help When Needed _____ 30
    Boosting Test Scores _____ 33
    Test-Taking Strategies _____ 33
    Maintaining Good Health during Exams _____ 34
    Celebrating Success and Setting Future Goals _____ 35
    Start Today _____ 36

Chapter 3: Managing Your Money Wisely _____ *37*
    Budgeting and Financial Literacy _____ 38
    The Importance of Budgeting _____ 38
    Understanding Income and Expenses _____ 39
    Creating a Practical Budget _____ 40
    Avoiding Common Financial Pitfalls _____ 41
    Saving and Investing _____ 43

    Investing Basics _____ 43
    The Power of Saving _____ 44
    Simple Investment Options for Teens _____ 45
    Financial Goals and Planning _____ 45
    Earning More Money _____ 46
    Exploring Part-Time Jobs and Freelancing _____ 47
    Balancing Work and School_____ 48
    Start Today _____ 50

Chapter 4: Decision-Making and Problem Solving _____ 53
    Accessing Options _____ 54
    Decision-Making Process _____ 56
    Problem-Solving Strategies _____ 58
    Resilience and Coping Mechanisms _____ 60
    Start Today _____ 63

Chapter 5: Effective Communication Skills _____ 65
    Active Listening and Empathy_____ 66
    Assertiveness vs. Aggressiveness _____ 67
    Assertiveness: _____ 68
    Aggressiveness _____ 69
    Finding the Right Balance: _____ 70
    Nonverbal Communication _____ 71
    Body Language _____ 72
    Facial Expressions _____ 72
    Gestures _____ 72
    Tone of Voice _____ 73
    Eye Contact _____ 73
    Proxemics _____ 73
    Conflict Resolution for Teens _____ 74
    Building Healthy Friendships _____ 77
    Start Today _____ 79

Chapter 6: Setting and Achieving Goals _____ 82
    Defining S.M.A.R.T. Goals _____ 83
    Specific _____ 83
    Measurable _____ 84
    Achievable _____ 84
    Relevant_____ 84
    Time-bound_____ 84
    Put into action _____ 85
    Overcoming Obstacles and Staying Motivated _____ 85
    Tracking Progress _____ 87
    Celebrating Success_____ 90

- Adjusting Your Goals over Time _____ 92
- Start Today _____ 94

Chapter 7: Emotional Intelligence and Self-Awareness _____ 98
- Identifying and Managing Emotions _____ 98
- Building Resilience _____ 100
- Self-Reflection and Self-Regulation _____ 102
- Empathy towards Others _____ 104
- Conflict Resolution _____ 105
- Self-Awareness: _____ 106
- Empathy: _____ 106
- Self-Regulation: _____ 107
- Effective Communication: _____ 107
- Collaborative Approach: _____ 107
- Strategic Disengagement: _____ 108
- Start Today _____ 108

Chapter 8: Peer Pressure and Healthy Relationships _____ 112
- Recognizing Positive and Negative Peer Pressure _____ 113
- Saying No _____ 115
- Boundaries and Respect _____ 117

Chapter 9: Bringing It All Together _____ 122
- Developing a Personal Action Plan _____ 122
- Seeking Mentorship and Guidance _____ 124
- Inspiration _____ 127

Final Words _____ 130

Références _____ 133

Chapter 1: Building Self-Esteem and Confidence

"To love oneself is the beginning of a life-long romance." Oscar Wilde

Dear Diary,

Ugh, today was like any other day—feeling invisible, not cool or smart enough, surrounded by people who seem to have their lives together, especially on freaking Instagram. But guess what? Something actually interesting happened!

I stumbled into the library to escape the chaos, and there was Mr. Peterson, the librarian who's basically a chill chess ninja. He convinced me to play, even though I'm rusty as heck. And you know what? He dropped some serious life lessons during those games. Like, every piece on the chessboard matters, just like every person has something special. Suddenly, I started thinking, maybe I'm not as lame as I thought.

So, with each game, I got better and started feeling kinda bold. I even started answering questions in class and joined the chess club. Who knew moving pieces on a chessboard could be like making moves in life?

And guess what else? The talent show is coming up, and I did something totally wild—I signed up! Not for chess, though. I'm gonna spill my guts on stage with some poetry about being okay with who you are. Can you believe it?

Growing as a person is the first step on the path to success. For teens, this trip isn't just about reaching outside goals; it's also about growing and discovering who they are.

Personal growth is a strong tool teens can use to reach their full potential, get past problems, and make their futures. You need to know who you are, where you want to go, and how to become the person who can get there. In this chapter, teens are encouraged to start this life-changing journey, with the idea that they often grow the most during the tough times and changes of adolescence. The power of personal growth comes in its ability to make you more open to new opportunities, stronger, and more likely to be successful in the future.

Self-Esteem

Understanding Self-Esteem

Your sense of self-worth is the silent judge of your performance in life. It works as an objective judge of how well you're doing. When you are feeling positive about yourself, it's as if an inner cheerleader is praising your every action. But when it's low, it's like an inner critic is booing and criticizing your every move. This is especially important for young adults to understand since self-esteem impacts everything from academic performance to social interactions to the way one deals with adversities.

Think about self-esteem like your mental muscle. It may be weak or strong, like your biceps or abs, and it becomes stronger with a workout. The ability to appreciate oneself enough to make self-serving decisions is an essential part of healthy self-esteem. It's similar to putting on a set of glasses that magnify your strengths and highlight your weaknesses so you can make improvements without being hard on yourself.

But here's the thing—self-esteem isn't static. Things might shift from day to day and even from moment to moment. You might go from feeling on top of the world since you aced a presentation to feeling depressed because you missed an idea in a discussion. This is typical. What's crucial is learning to control these phases of life so the lows don't knock you out and the highs don't take you away into overconfidence.

The Impact of Self-Esteem on Life

Believing in your abilities is nothing short of a superpower, with far-reaching effects that touch every aspect of your life. It wields a profound influence, starting with your capacity to confront challenges head-on, bolstering your resilience. Shifting your perspective from "I can't do this" to "I've got this" represents a monumental shift, whether you're gearing up for a daunting exam or addressing a demanding audience, like during a school assembly. Self-assured individuals are also less likely to conform to the crowd when their principles differ. It's akin to having an anchor to cling to when faced with adversity.

Moreover, this power isn't confined to monumental moments alone; it subtly guides your everyday choices. It nudges you towards choosing a nourishing meal because you prioritize your well-being or waking up early to study because you firmly believe in the value of your future. As an added perk, it encourages you to save money rather than fritter it away on unnecessary expenditures. This distinction lies between actively shaping your destiny and passively waiting for it to unfold.

Identifying Areas for Improvement

Self-respect is not inherent; it must be developed like any other ability. To get there, you must first know your starting point. Think about the things you excel in and those you may be satisfied with. Perhaps you have a natural talent for making other people laugh or are an intellectual genius. These are the things you may feel good about in yourself. Next, think about the regions where you're not feeling so good. Maybe you become anxious when doing math or when meeting strangers. There's no need to worry; everybody has challenges in life. These are merely the areas where you can level up.

Increasing your confidence level is something that takes time. You may work on your social skills by making a point of saying hello to one new person every week or on your math abilities by starting a study group. Every time you accomplish one of these targets, it's like a victory for your team. You'll feel stronger and more able as your confidence in yourself grows with each victory.

So, knowing how to boost your self-esteem isn't simply as important as learning how to feel good about yourself in the first place. It's about recognizing that you have this, even when circumstances are rough. Simply put, nobody can stop you if you have faith in yourself.

Case Study

Emma's Journey to Boosted Self-Esteem

So, guess what happened today in my 17-year-old life? You know, I'm that junior in high school who usually keeps things low-key. People see me as quiet, never really jumping into classroom chatter. It's not like I'm not smart, but this constant self-doubt makes me feel like I'm playing catch-up with my classmates.

But today was different. My English teacher, Ms. Turner, noticed my writing skills. She decided to throw me into the spotlight during class discussions. At first, making these small contributions was nerve-wracking, but Ms. Turner was all for it. She pushed me to keep going. And get this – my parents, sensing my struggles, brought in this counsellor who's all about boosting teen self-esteem. Like, what?

Through some classes and strategies, I'm starting to see my strengths. It's wild how the support from my family and the counsellor is making a difference. Today, I took a leap and joined the debate club. Total game-changer. My confidence is growing, and I'm seeing my own value through what I bring to the team.

Slowly, my self-worth is on the rise. I'm not just speaking up in class but diving into after-school activities. My connections with people are getting real more open. I decided to run for the student council – talk about a nerve-wracking move. Even though I don't know how it'll turn out, just the act of trying is giving my self-worth a major boost. Oh, and guess what? I actually won the election. Can you believe it?

As I'm nearing graduation, it's crazy to think about the shift in me. I'm not that same insecure kid anymore. I've grown some serious self-esteem. From dodging challenges, I'm now facing them head-on. My story is all about having a solid support crew, a game plan, and learning to believe in myself.

Speaking of cool stories, let me tell you about my cousin Lily. She's not the academic type either, and she used to think she was less bright than her siblings. But turns out she's got this insane talent for connecting with animals. Today, she shared how she started helping out at the local animal shelter at 15. Her unique brilliance shines through, calming even the wildest animals. That boost in confidence helped her see she was just as smart as her siblings, just in her own awesome way.

Personal Anecdote

Lily, my cousin, always stood out within our family, but not in the way one might expect. She carried a quiet demeanor and often found herself in the shadows of her academically successful brothers. Lily's self-perception suffered as she believed she didn't measure up in terms of intelligence. Little did we know, she possessed an extraordinary gift that set her apart: an unparalleled ability to connect with animals.

I vividly recall her sharing stories from her time as a volunteer at the local animal shelter when she was around 15 years old. It was there that her unique brilliance began to shine through. With her gentle touch and soothing words, Lily possessed an innate talent for calming even the most terrified stray dogs and pets. She worked wonders with these animals, transforming them in remarkable ways.

The shelter staff swiftly recognized the positive impact Lily had on the animals. Her presence had a soothing effect, making them more content and approachable, ultimately increasing their chances of finding loving homes. This transformation wasn't solely a triumph for the animals; it marked a significant turning point for Lily herself.

During her time at the shelter, Lily learned a profound lesson about the diverse forms of talent. She came to understand that her ability to connect with and communicate with animals was a unique form of brilliance, every bit as genuine and substantial as excelling in traditional subjects at school. This newfound awareness boosted her confidence and led her to truly appreciate her distinctive skills.

Lily's story imparted a crucial lesson to me about the various types of intelligence and the importance of recognizing and valuing our individual abilities. I will forever admire and take pride in her journey of self-discovery and the incredible difference she made in the lives of those animals.

Self-Compassion

Building a Positive Self-Image

The process of creating a positive image of oneself is analogous to establishing a garden. It won't happen quickly, and you'll have to give it some time daily, but the result is a stunning sight to see. Begin by developing positive attitudes about yourself as a starting point. Instead of dwelling on what you perceive to be shortcomings, pay attention to the aspects of yourself that you enjoy. Perhaps you have excellent listening skills, are an innovative thinker, or are a dependable friend. These characteristics are your flowers; if you focus on them, they'll blossom into something beautiful.

Your mind may be like a camera, frequently taking snapshots of your errors and the awful days you've had. It's time to switch lenses and begin grabbing the opportunities to take pictures of the wonderful times. Take a moment to relish your success, no matter how minor the accomplishment may seem. This might be anything as simple as being on time to work, bringing a smile to someone else's face, or completing a task you've been putting off. Enjoy your victories, and you'll find that your perception of yourself will start to improve.

Developing Self-Compassion

Self-compassion is the art of extending kindness to yourself while acknowledging that making mistakes is a fundamental part of our human experience. Instead of becoming your harshest critic when you stumble, aim to be your strongest ally. Treat yourself with the same empathy and understanding you'd offer to a close friend or a beloved family member. If a friend received a failing grade on an exam, you wouldn't berate them with, "Well, you're a failure." Instead, you'd likely respond with words like, "It's okay. You'll do better next time." Extend that same gentleness to yourself.

Mindfulness meditation stands as a valuable tool for cultivating self-compassion. It involves being fully present in the moment and embracing your emotions without judgment. Rather than trying to push away negative feelings when you're down, imagine sitting with them. Dive into the reasons behind your current emotional state and remember that it's perfectly acceptable to acknowledge when you're not feeling your best. Simply recognizing and allowing yourself to experience your emotions marks the initial step toward healing and self-compassion.

Setting and Achieving Goals

Think of your goals as the destination on your personal journey along an open road. Just like any trip, you'll require a map (representing your plan), a few waypoints (symbolizing short-term aims), and your ultimate destination (your long-term goal). Start small to prevent feeling overwhelmed. For instance, if your aim is to improve your fitness, beginning with a ten-minute daily walk is a more manageable start than preparing for a marathon. These are essential baby steps, and achieving each checkpoint will give your self-esteem a well-deserved boost.

The SMART acronym, which stands for Specific, Measurable, Achievable, Relevant, and Time-bound, is a valuable tool when setting goals. Instead of a vague statement like "I want to get better at math," make it more concrete: "I will dedicate 30 minutes to math practice every day to raise my grade by one letter within three months." This way, you'll have a clear understanding of what you want to achieve and when you aim to achieve it.

Remember to stay adaptable. Just like in any journey, road closures or unexpected weather changes might force you to take a different route. It's perfectly acceptable for your plan to encounter obstacles along the way. You may need to make adjustments, but always keep your ultimate goal in sight.

By integrating these strategies, you'll lay the groundwork for a strong foundation of self-esteem. Cultivating a positive self-image, practicing self-compassion, and diligently pursuing your goals are like the essential elements of light, water, and soil for plant growth. If you remain patient and put in the necessary effort, not only will you make significant progress toward your objectives, but you'll also discover that the journey itself is enjoyable, enhancing your self-esteem along the way.

Recognizing Self-Doubt Patterns

Self-doubt may be like a cunning little gremlin, appearing when you are least expecting it and taking you by surprise. It's like that old song you remember so well that keeps playing in your brain, reminding you that you can't accomplish something or aren't sufficiently talented to do it. However, in order to put an end to this unpleasant music, you will first need to become familiar with the lyrics. The first step in changing the song is to become aware of the patterns of self-doubt that you engage in.

Take note of the moments in which you question your decisions and judgments. Is it when you're venturing into uncharted territory? Or perhaps when you're in the presence of specific people? These items are hints. You may have noticed that if you screw up, you immediately start to believe that your life is a total and utter loss. That is not the truth. Instead, it's your own self-doubt speaking through you. As soon as you identify these patterns, you will be able to avoid yourself from falling into the trap.

Overcoming Negative Self-Talk

Learning how to overcome negative self-talk may be compared to discovering how to dance. You could trip over your feet when you first start dancing, but you can glide around the dance floor after a few lessons. The trick is to vary your steps in different ways. If you find that you are stating "I can't," try rephrasing it as "I can't yet, but I'm trying." Be kind to yourself and recognize that you are a work in progress.

It's also important not to give your inner critic a chance to dominate the debate. Turn the volume off as soon as it begins to chime in with "You're going to mess this up," and then tell yourself of the instances that you have succeeded in the past. If you need to, compile a list of everything you can be glad about. Keep this list on hand for moments when you want a jolt of inspiration to remind you of how wonderful you are.

Seeking Support and Mentorship

Everybody needs someone who supports them even when they are having trouble believing in themselves. Seeking out help and mentoring is similar to hiring the services of a self-esteem coach or personal trainer. It's important that you surround yourself with people who recognize your potential and push you to go after your goals and ambitions.

This person might be a professor, a coach, a member of the family, or simply a friend. These individuals will support you and guide you along the way. They are the individuals who will give you that motivational boost when you're feeling low, who will help you organize when you're confronting a task, and who will rejoice with you when you overcome it after you've accomplished it.

Do not be hesitant to reach out to others and seek their opinions or suggestions. Conversing with someone who has been in the same boat might sometimes provide you with a new point of view. Also, keep in mind that asking for help is not a sign of weakness; rather, it is a wise technique for anybody who wants to improve their self-esteem and conquer their feelings of self-doubt.

"The worst loneliness is to not be comfortable with yourself." Mark Twain

Start Today:

- Start today by recognizing your abilities and accepting that your flaws make you who you are.
- Set new tasks or goals for yourself that will push you and boost your confidence as you reach them.
- Celebrate your small wins every day.

In the following chapters, we'll dive deeper into specific life skills that will shape your future.

Which of the following are your strengths? Which ones need improvement?

Great Talker: Leader in the Making: I know how to take charge and inspire others to join in on the fun.

Team Player: I love working with my buddies to get things done together.

Quick Learner: Whether it's a new game or a school subject, I pick up things super-fast.

Problem-Solving Whiz: I'm like a detective—good at figuring out tricky stuff and finding solutions.

Time Master: I can juggle lots of things at once and still get everything done on time.

Initiative Taker: I'm proactive in initiating new activities and contributing to tasks at home or in the community.

Idea Generator: My brain is always buzzing with new and cool ideas.

Mr./Ms. Reliable: When I say I'll do something, you can count on me to get it done.

Bounce-Back Champ: I'm really good at turning things around and staying positive.

Super Detail-Oriented: I notice all the little things to make sure everything is just right.

Peacekeeper: I'm good at helping my friends work things out and finding solutions to problems.

Organizational Wizard: I excel at keeping my school materials and living space neat and well-organized.

Study Guru: I'm dedicated to discovering effective study techniques and optimizing my homework routine.

Master Communicator: I'm actively working on expressing my thoughts and emotions more clearly and confidently.

Attentive Listener: I'm actively developing my ability to listen attentively and understand others.

Tech Savvy with Boundaries: I'm mindful of my screen time, maintaining a healthy relationship with technology.

Champion of Healthy Living: I prioritize a well-balanced diet, regular exercise, and quality sleep for a healthy lifestyle.

Confidence Architect: I'm building my self-confidence and embracing belief in my capabilities.

Stress Management Maestro: I'm developing effective strategies for handling and mitigating stress in various situations.

Create a schedule of tasks to stay updated, ontime and organized.

"Failing to plan is planning to fail" Benjamin Franklin

Search on Google for 'apps to help plan my day and week', and you will find many solutions to help organize the day, week, month and year.

Three suggestions:

- Google Calendar: Free and integrates well with other apps
- TickTick: Free version with student/teacher discount on the paid version Todist: Free version
- Evernote: Free version

Of course, you could go old school and just keep a notebook or diary.

Chapter 2: Acing your Exams

Did you know? A comprehensive study by Harvard University found that over 70% of teenagers suffer from significant stress during exams, mirroring clinical anxiety level

Often, teens are in a "time crunch dilemma" because of how quickly life moves these days. College, extracurricular events, social responsibilities, and personal hobbies all want their limited time. This chapter discusses teens' problems when trying to manage their time well. Setting realistic goals, setting priorities, and finding a balance between work and free time are all things that show how important it is. Even though this problem is tough, it also gives teens a chance to learn important life skills like handling their time, making decisions, and dealing with stress. The goal is to give kids ways to deal with this problem to make the most of their time without risking their health or personal growth.

Exams are a vital part of a student's educational journey, but they also bring with them a wave of anxiety that can make even the most conscientious students feel helpless. If not properly managed, this stress can have a negative impact not just on a person's academic achievement but also on their mental and emotional well-being.

Exams don't have to be a cause of anxiety as long as students go into them with the appropriate mindset. Exam stress can be a significant obstacle, but with the help of this guide, it can be transformed into a part of your academic life that is more manageable and can be understood. We will discuss ways to manage stress, enhance your confidence, and study habits that can help you learn more efficiently.

By making use of these resources, you will not only be able to lessen the negative effects of exam stress but also improve your performance on the tests themselves. It is important to keep in mind that excelling on your examinations requires more than simply memorizing knowledge; rather, it requires developing an attitude that combines being well-prepared, maintaining a positive outlook, and remaining resilient.

Let's start on this road to transform the anxiety of exams into success.

Effective Study Techniques

It takes more than determination and hard work to succeed in school; you must also employ efficient study methods. These methods equip pupils with the means to absorb, process, and memorize knowledge more effectively and efficiently. In a world where there is so much to discover but so little time, it is absolutely necessary to be able to study in an effective way.

There are many aspects to consider while discussing efficient study methods. It is not enough to just spend hours poring over books and lecture notes; rather, one has to maximize the value of those hours in order to achieve the most desirable results. This requires first gaining an awareness of how the brain absorbs and remembers information and then developing a set of study habits that are aligned with that understanding of how the brain works. Using efficient study techniques helps to break down difficult information into more manageable chunks, making the learning process feel less daunting and more achievable.

Time management and study schedules.

Embarking on an educational journey necessitates the development of productive study habits, which are essential for achieving academic success. Effective time management and the organization of study schedules are the cornerstones of these habits and significantly contribute to their effectiveness. When it comes to managing your time effectively for academic pursuits, the key is not to overload your schedule with as many tasks as possible. Instead, it's about methodically structuring your time and prioritizing tasks to maximize the productivity of your study sessions.

Think of effective time management as a form of art, where each step of preparation contributes to the creation of a masterpiece that reflects your educational experience. It all begins with a straightforward process: assessing the time available during your week and then allocating it in alignment with your academic goals. This approach breaks down the daunting task of covering an entire curriculum into manageable and focused study periods.

Creating a study schedule is akin to charting a course for a treasure hunt. It guides you systematically through the labyrinth of your coursework, ensuring you allocate appropriate time to each topic or subject. However, it's important to remember that flexibility is crucial for a productive study routine. Your schedule should be adaptable enough to accommodate unexpected twists and turns that life may throw your way.

Active Learning

Active learning surpasses passive information absorption by a significant margin. It requires you to personally engage with the material, analyze it, and apply it in various contexts. This approach transforms the act of learning from a mundane task into an exciting and enjoyable experience.

Think about how you approach class discussions and lessons. Engaging in conversations about a subject or teaching it to someone else forces you to revisit the content, strengthen your understanding, and identify areas that need more attention. Explaining ideas to others is a powerful technique that reinforces your own learning.

Visual aids like mind maps and flashcards are indispensable tools in active learning. A mind map visually connects different pieces of knowledge around a central theme, making it ideal for visual learners. Flashcards, on the other hand, are excellent for memorizing information such as definitions and statistics. They promote active recall, which actively stimulates your memory as you learn something new.

Incorporating quizzes and practice exams into your study routine is another effective active learning strategy.

These tools not only familiarize you with the exam format but also enhance your ability to remember and comprehend information.

Active note-taking goes beyond simply transcribing what you read or hear. It involves processing the information, summarizing it in your own words, asking questions about it, and making connections to other ideas. This approach ensures that you're not passively recording information but actively engaging with it.

Efficient study methods combine well-organized time management strategies with dynamic active learning approaches. By mastering these techniques, you can turn your study time into engaging and meaningful experiences that pave the path to academic success. Remember, consistency and adaptability are the two most crucial elements in effective learning.

Mindful Studying

Maximizing your potential to absorb knowledge and improving your educational experience can be achieved through mindful studying and focus. This strategy isn't just about memorizing information; it's about being fully present and immersed in the learning process, enhancing the quality of your study sessions.

The first step in practicing mindful learning is to have a heightened awareness of your immediate surroundings. It involves recognizing when your mind wanders and gently bringing it back to your task so that you can focus on what you're supposed to be doing. While this practice may seem straightforward, it's a powerful tool for efficient learning. When you study mindfully, you're not simply skimming through content; you're actively interacting with it, analyzing it, and questioning what you've learned, which deepens your understanding of the subject matter.

The setting in which you study significantly impacts your ability to concentrate. Identifying or creating an environment that aligns with your study goals and minimizes distractions is crucial. This doesn't necessarily mean complete silence or isolation. It's about being mindful of what environment enhances your focus. For some, the ideal setting is a quiet space with minimal distractions, while for others, the ambient noise of a bustling coffee shop unexpectedly boosts productive thinking. The key is to be aware of what atmosphere maximizes your ability to focus and then tailor your study space accordingly.

Techniques to Enhance Focus

The inclusion of certain strategies that boost focus improves mindful studying. One of these methods is to begin your time spent studying with a few minutes of slow, deep breathing or a brief period of mindfulness meditation. This routine will assist in calming your mind and getting it ready for the task that lies ahead. One more productive method, the Pomodoro Technique, involves studying in intense bursts of activity interspersed with brief intervals of rest. A high level of concentration can be maintained with the help of this strategy, which additionally assists in avoiding burnout.

Another important component of mindful studying involves concentrating on one thing at a time. In a world that often celebrates the advantages of multitasking, making the conscious decision to concentrate on one task at a time during your study sessions can greatly boost the productivity of those sessions. It enables you to completely submerge yourself in the topic at hand, which eventually results in deeper understanding and improved memory.

Self-compassion is an important aspect of mindful studying that is sometimes neglected. It is essential to have the mindset that staying focused can be difficult at times and that it is natural for your thoughts to stray from time to time. The goal of mindful studying is not to achieve a perfect focus; rather, it is to recognize when you have become distracted from your studies and bring your attention back to them in a calm and composed manner. It requires that you treat yourself with compassion and remain patient throughout this process. Every instance in which you find yourself distracted is a chance to redirect your attention to where it ought to be.

Studying mindfully is more than just picking up new information; it is about developing an in-depth and lasting engagement with the content that you are studying. You may make your time spent studying more productive and pleasurable by providing yourself with an encouraging environment, employing strategies that improve attention, and cultivating self-compassion. Your educational experience as a whole will be improved by adopting this mindful approach.

My friend Jamie once shared with me an inspiring story about his academic breakthrough. We were sitting in our usual spot at the neighborhood café, sipping coffee, and he began recounting the challenges he had faced and the strategies that had turned his academic journey around.

"Remember how I used to drown in notes and books but still struggled to improve my grades?" Jamie started, absently stirring his coffee. He had always been a diligent worker, yet his efforts never seemed to yield the desired results.

"Well, then I discovered mindful studying, and it changed everything," he continued. At first, this technique appeared deceptively simple, almost like paying close attention in class and avoiding daydreaming. But believe me, it made a world of difference.

I recalled Jamie's battles with distractions and his habit of multitasking, which had ultimately led to his burnout. Seeing him now, more composed and self-assured, was truly remarkable.

Jamie added, "And then there was time management." "I used to think that pulling all-nighters was the best approach to studying. However, establishing a structured study schedule with designated time slots for each subject made a significant impact. It became clear that the quality of study time mattered more than the quantity."

Watching Jamie's transformation was truly inspiring. He had evolved from someone constantly worried about his grades to a person who had mastered the art of effective studying. His story was about more than just academic improvement; it was a testament to developing a well-rounded and thoughtful approach to education and life.

Avoiding Procrastination

Mastering the art of avoiding procrastination is a skill that can enhance productivity and reduce stress levels. To succeed, it's crucial to tackle tasks promptly, even if they initially seem challenging or uninteresting. Delaying work until the last minute often leads to rushed efforts, compromising the quality of your work and increasing stress.

To begin, break down large tasks into smaller, manageable segments. This approach not only makes getting started less intimidating but also provides a sense of accomplishment as you complete each portion. It transforms an overwhelming task into a series of achievable steps.

Another effective strategy is to establish clear goals. Precisely defining what needs to be done and documenting it helps maintain focus, improve time management, track progress, and stay on course.

Creating a plan is a key element in avoiding procrastination. Allocate specific time slots for each task and strive to adhere to this plan as closely as possible. Designating dedicated work periods can prevent last-minute procrastination and instill a sense of responsibility and routine.

Identifying your motivation is crucial. Reflect on the reasons behind completing a task. Understanding the "why" can provide the drive needed to start and finish it, whether it's to earn a good grade, acquire new knowledge, or fulfill a responsibility.

Minimizing distractions plays a pivotal role. Choose a quiet workspace and remove any gadgets or mobile phones that may divert your attention. A distraction-free environment fosters concentration and task completion.

Lastly, rewarding yourself upon finishing a task or a portion of it can provide motivation to keep going. This reward could be a short break, a special treat, or some personal time. It creates an incentive to look forward to and makes working on tasks more enjoyable.

It's important to remember that making occasional mistakes is normal. Be kind to yourself and keep moving forward. Consistently applying these strategies will gradually make it easier to avoid procrastination, resulting in more productive days and reduced stress levels.

Dealing with Exam Anxiety

Exam anxiety has been around for as long as there have been exams themselves. The closer an examination gets, the more you notice a flutter in your stomach, a racing heart, and a buzzing head. The successful management of this anxiety is important not only for achieving educational objectives but also for protecting one's mental and emotional health. This section will discuss how to handle the harsh seas of exam stress.

Strategies for Managing Stress

Finding strategies that work for you is the key to effectively managing the stress linked to exams. The first step in doing so is being able recognize the early warning signs of stress. Are you more irritable than you usually are? Have difficulties falling or staying asleep? It's possible that your body is trying to tell you to calm down and take better care of yourself by displaying. Techniques of mindfulness and relaxation can be of tremendous assistance at times. You can concentrate your thoughts and soothe your nerves by meditating for only a few minutes or doing some simple breathing techniques. Another effective method for relieving stress involves participating in physical activity. There is no need for it to be a rigorous workout; even something as simple as taking a leisurely stroll or a session of mild yoga can do wonders for clearing your thoughts and easing tension.

Making a comprehensive study schedule is another essential step in effective stress management. Try splitting up your study time into manageable portions rather than subjecting yourself to extended, challenging study sessions. It helps to minimize the feeling of being overburdened with content. Keep in mind that your brain requires rest in order to absorb and process new knowledge properly.

Test Preparation and Organization

Exam anxiety often stems from a feeling of being ill-prepared, and the key to performing well on an exam is directly linked to the structure and systemization of your preparation. To combat this anxiety, it's essential to take a methodical approach to your exam readiness.

Start by gathering all the necessary information about the exam, including its format, the most pertinent concepts, and the types of questions that may be asked. This groundwork makes it easier to establish clear educational goals.

Following this, it's crucial to organize the material you've been studying. Ensure your notes are well-structured and easily accessible. For complex subjects, consider creating summaries or mental maps. If you're a visual learner, try employing color-coded charts or notes. Practice with past papers or take mock tests to familiarize yourself with the exam format. Not only does this aid in comprehending the structure of the exam, but it also enhances your time management skills during the actual test.

Avoid the temptation to procrastinate and cram at the last minute. Cramming can exacerbate anxiety and has minimal impact on long-term knowledge retention. Instead, engage in regular review activities to solidify your understanding of the material.

Seeking Help When Needed

Exam anxiety can often feel overwhelming, even when you are doing everything in your capacity to avoid it. When this happens, it is important to look for assistance. A smart way to get started is by having a conversation with students, friends, or family. They may be going through something similar themselves and are able to offer support or advice to those who are.

If your anxiety is having a significant impact on your day-to-day life or the way you normally study, you might think about getting some professional assistance. Counsellors and therapists are able to suggest solutions that can help clients better manage their anxiety. In addition, a large number of educational institutions provide resources for the management of stress as well as counselling services. Do not be hesitant to make use of these available resources. Keep in mind that asking for assistance is a sign of strength, not weakness.

Understanding and learning how to manage your stress, being well-organized in your test preparation, and acknowledging when you need assistance are the keys to successfully coping with exam anxiety. Not only does each of these facets play an important role in overcoming exam anxiety, but they also play an important role in establishing a healthier approach to learning and exams. It's all about striking a balance, where you challenge yourself to perform at your best without jeopardizing your health and happiness in the process. Remember that it's alright to feel pressured, that it's normal to be nervous, but that with the appropriate tactics and support, you can emerge successful and more resilient than before. As you progress through your academic journey, keep in mind that it's okay to be stressed that it's normal to be anxious.

"Ask for help not because you're weak, but because you want to remain strong."

Emma and I have been friends since the beginning of our first year of college, and if there is one remarkable thing about her, it's her battle with exam anxiety. Her journey of overcoming it has left a lasting impression on me.

During our senior year, as we approached graduation, I noticed a significant change in Emma. While she had always been diligent, the stress she felt during exam periods seemed to intensify. However, that year, she made a resolute decision to confront her anxieties head-on.

Emma began by acknowledging the immense pressure she was under. "I can't let this control me anymore," she declared. She initiated a practice of mindfulness, incorporating meditation and focused breathing into her daily routine. It was remarkable to witness how these brief moments of respite from her busy schedule made a profound difference in her mental well-being.

What truly astonished me was her willingness to seek help when needed. Emma, who had a history of handling challenges independently, took the bold step of joining a study group. It seemed that sharing her concerns and listening to others who faced similar struggles made her feel less isolated.

On our final exam day, the results of Emma's hard work were evident to everyone. She, who had previously been easily agitated, displayed a remarkable level of composure. With a smile, she simply said, "I've done my best."

Emma's journey isn't just about conquering her exam anxiety and becoming more self-reliant. It was a profound transformation from a stressed-out student to someone who could manage her anxieties with grace. Her experience exemplified the power that comes from acknowledging challenges, implementing effective techniques, and seeking assistance when necessary. Emma's triumph over exam anxiety not only led to academic success but also instilled in her a newfound confidence that radiated in all aspects of her life.

"You don't have to control your thoughts; you just have to stop letting them control you."

Boosting Test Scores

Many students aim to improve their exam results, but accomplishing this requires more than just understanding the content of the courses they take. It is about adopting a holistic strategy that covers effective test-taking methods, keeping good health during examinations, and acknowledging accomplishments to set future goals. Let's go deeper into these components to better understand how they work together to boost students' performance on standardized tests and improve the educational experience as a whole.

Test-Taking Strategies

The ability to master test-taking procedures is analogous to possessing a toolkit since it enables one to navigate through examinations with self-assurance and efficiency. The effective management of time throughout the exam is an essential technique. It is essential to manage your time well, taking the appropriate amount of time on each question and avoiding becoming bogged down for an extended period of time on more challenging questions. Another essential tactic is being familiar with the structure of the examination and preparing for it accordingly. For example, responding to essay questions requires a very different strategy from responding to multiple-choice questions.

It is really important to thoroughly read the instructions and comprehend what is being asked in each question. When students are pressed for time during an exam, they may overlook important nuances in the questions. It is a good habit to quickly go back over your answers and check to see if they correspond to the questions that were asked.

Your performance can be considerably improved by using strategies such as elimination while answering multiple-choice questions or outlining your views before writing an essay. These techniques will assist you in organizing your thoughts and ensure that your responses are succinct while still addressing the question at hand.

Maintaining Good Health during Exams

It is very important to keep one's health in good condition when studying for exams. Your mental and physical health has an immediate and direct influence on your capacity for performance. The importance of getting enough sleep, maintaining a balanced diet, and drinking enough water cannot be overstated. Because sleep deprivation can have a negative impact on both memory and concentration, maintaining a consistent sleep pattern in the days leading up to and during your tests is essential.

The benefits of exercise can be enormous, even when only a little exercise is done. Not only does it keep you physically fit, but it also lessens the effects of stress and makes your mind clearer. Remember that maintaining a healthy body helps maintain a healthy mind, which is necessary for doing well on tests.

Stress management is an important component in overall health maintenance. Exam anxiety can be managed to some extent via the practice of techniques such as mindfulness, meditation, or even straightforward breathing exercises. It is essential to take little rests between studying periods to refresh and revitalize your thoughts.

Celebrating Success and Setting Future Goals

Regardless of your test results, it's crucial to acknowledge and celebrate your accomplishments. This boosts morale and helps assess which strategies and techniques worked and which didn't. Learning from both your successes and failures provides valuable insights for future tests.

The process begins with setting goals for the future. Planning ahead and identifying the steps needed to continuously improve is essential. Goal-setting encompasses not only academic achievements but also personal and professional development. You might want to enhance your time management skills or focus on challenging subjects.

Remember that goals should be SMART: specific, measurable, attainable, relevant, and time-bound. Using this framework makes it easier to define clear and achievable objectives. Moreover, keep in mind that goals should be flexible and adaptable to the ever-changing demands of life.

Improving test scores requires a multifaceted approach that goes beyond simply mastering course content. It involves effective test-taking strategies, prioritizing both physical and mental well-being, celebrating successes, and setting goals for the future. Embracing these elements allows students not only to elevate their test scores but also to cultivate skills and routines that will serve them well throughout their educational and professional journeys. The path to academic success is an ongoing one, with each stage offering opportunities for growth and progress.

Start Today

- Now is the time to think about how you spend your time and make a plan for your days with clear goals.

- Use schedules or apps to keep track of your time today to keep your tasks organized and your progress visible.

- Make a commitment to yourself to start using your time management and organization techniques on a regular basis.

Up next, we'll discuss financial responsibility, a crucial life skill.

Chapter 3: Managing Your Money Wisely

Did you know that a recent survey found that nearly 60% of teenagers in the United States admitted they have very little information about how to manage personal finances properly? This shocking fact sheds light on an essential knowledge gap in young individuals' financial literacy. Understanding and prudently managing one's financial resources is a talent that every teenager should strive to master in today's world. This chapter will walk you through the fundamentals of money management and assist you in laying a foundation that will serve you well into your adult years.

This journey inspires people, especially young people, to learn about personal finance, improve their spending habits, and discover smart ways to put their money to make it work for them. It's basically the idea that financial freedom isn't just for rich people; anyone who is willing to learn and use good money habits can get there. This journey isn't just about getting rich; it's also about getting the freedom and confidence that come with being financially stable.

Budgeting and Financial Literacy

Personal finance can be hard to understand, especially for people who are just starting out on their way to being financially independent. A strong understanding of budgeting and basic financial literacy is key to effective financial management. The purpose of this part is to simplify the process of budgeting by explaining its significance, providing guidance on how to strike a healthy balance between income and expenses, and outlining the procedures necessary to develop a workable budget.

The Importance of Budgeting

A budget is more than just a tool for managing money; it's a road map for accomplishing your goals and safeguarding your financial future. Budgeting is an essential part of personal financial management. It's important to be aware of where your money is going so you can make educated choices about how you use it. Learning how to create and stick to a budget is an essential life skill that should be developed by young people and teens. It teaches self-control and planning.

Your spending patterns and the things that are most important to you financially are reflected in a budget, which serves as a kind of financial mirror. It is helpful in identifying areas in which you may be spending more than necessary and possibilities in which you might save money. First and foremost, creating a budget gives you the ability to take charge of your financial situation and make proactive decisions rather than reactive ones. It prevents your money from dominating you while simultaneously giving you power over it.

Understanding Income and Expenses

Understanding your income and expenses is the first step in creating a budget for the household. Teenagers can make money in a variety of ways, including working part-time, receiving an allowance from their parents, or earning money from odd jobs. It is necessary to understand the precise amount of money that is coming.

The majority of people have difficulty when it comes to their expenses. It is simple to understate how much money we spend, particularly on little and routine purchases. When you want to keep track of your spending, you should divide it into two categories: those that are essential (such as food, transportation, or educational materials) and those that are not needed (such as entertainment or luxury products). The ability to differentiate between one's needs and wants is an essential aspect of effectively managing one's finances.

Being aware of the irregular expenses that don't happen on a monthly basis but can have a major impact on your budget, such as annual subscriptions or spending during the holidays, is an important part of understanding your expenses. If you plan ahead for these costs, you won't have to worry about them becoming a strain on your finances.

Creating a Practical Budget

Now, we find ourselves at the heart of budgeting: crafting a realistic and practical plan. It's not about depriving yourself of life's pleasures but rather ensuring that your spending habits are sustainable.

To get started, compile a list of all your sources of income and expenses. Next, determine how much of your total income will be allocated to each expense category. It's crucial to be realistic; an overly strict budget can be just as counterproductive as having no budget at all. Realism here means being honest with yourself.

The 50/30/20 rule is a valuable guideline that suggests allocating 50% of your income to essential expenses, 30% to non-essential expenditures, and 20% to either savings or debt repayment. However, these percentages can be adjusted to suit your specific situation and goals.

In the realm of financial planning, technology can be a helpful companion. There is a wide range of software, including mobile apps and online tools that can simplify the process of tracking your income and expenses.

Remember that your budget should be updated whenever there's a change in your financial situation. Regularly reviewing and adjusting your budget ensures that it continues to meet your needs and aspirations.

Having a financial plan and understanding money are essential aspects of money management. By grasping the significance of budgeting, gaining control over your income and expenses, and creating a realistic and actionable budget, you set yourself on the path to financial stability and independence. This journey is one of self-discipline and self-discovery, equipping you with the tools to make informed and confident financial decisions throughout your life.

Avoiding Common Financial Pitfalls

Avoiding common financial pitfalls is crucial for maintaining the health of your finances and achieving long-term financial stability. Financial missteps can be like traps that derail your financial plans and goals. By being aware and cautious, you can steer clear of these typical mistakes.

One of the most detrimental errors is not having a budget. Your budget serves as your financial roadmap. It helps you keep track of your money and ensures that you don't spend more than you earn. Without a budget, it's easy to lose control of your spending, potentially leading to debt. Begin by documenting your income and expenses, then establish reasonable limits for each category and stay within them.

Another common mistake is overusing credit cards. While credit cards can be a helpful tool for managing your finances, using them recklessly can lead to trouble. Late fees and high-interest rates can quickly accumulate. It's important to use credit cards wisely, paying off your bills in full each month and not exceeding what you can comfortably repay.

Lacking an emergency fund poses a significant financial risk. Unexpected events such as car repairs or medical expenses can be costly. Without an emergency fund, you may resort to high-interest loans or credit cards to cover these unforeseen costs. Aim to save enough money in a separate account to cover your living expenses for three to six months.

Investing without sufficient knowledge can result in substantial financial losses. Investing can be complex, and diving in without a solid understanding of the basics is unwise. Conduct thorough research, assess the risks, and consider seeking guidance from financial experts before making investment decisions.

Neglecting insurance is another mistake to avoid. Insurance is a crucial component of financial planning, safeguarding against unexpected losses. Ensure you have health, auto, home, and life insurance to protect yourself and your assets. Adequate insurance coverage provides peace of mind in case of illness, injury, or unforeseen events.

Finally, failing to plan for retirement is a common oversight. It's advisable to start saving for retirement early, utilizing retirement savings plans like 401(k)s and IRAs. Compound interest means that even modest, regular contributions can grow significantly over time.

By paying attention to these areas—maintaining a budget, using credit cards responsibly, establishing an emergency fund, gaining investment knowledge, securing adequate insurance, and planning for retirement—you can avoid financial mistakes and work toward a secure financial future.

Saving and Investing

When it comes to personal finance, saving money and spending are two important things that hold financial growth and security together. Teenagers who start this process early can make good financial choices for the rest of their lives. This part is meant to teach you about the power of saving, look at some easy investments that teens can make, and show you how important it is to set financial goals and plan for the future.

Investing Basics

Investing may look hard, but the goal is to grow your money. Think of it as putting down a seed. It may start small but could develop into something much bigger over time. Putting your money into stocks, bonds, or real estate with the hope that they will be valued more in the future is what investment is all about.

First, let's talk about stocks. You get a small part of a company when you buy stocks. Your piece may become more valuable if the business does well. However, the value could go down if the business doesn't do well. It's kind of like having a stake in a business.

Bonds aren't the same. When you buy a bond, you give money to a business or the government. They promise to pay you back later and give you some extra money as a thank you. It's the same as lending money and getting interest.

One more way to invest is in real estate. This means buying homes or apartments to make money later by renting them out or selling them for more than you paid.

Putting money into investments is a good way to get rich, but there are risks involved. The money you put in can go up and down in value. Because of this, you should consider how long you want to invest and how much danger you will take. Don't forget that the best way to start spending is to learn about it and go slowly.

The Power of Saving

Saving money is a habit that can be formed at a young age. It's not enough to just save some of your allowance or money; you need to know how important it is to wait to get what you want. When you save, you're choosing to put your future needs and goals ahead of your wants right now. This skill is very important for planning your finances.

The simple act of saving and the idea of compound interest makes it so appealing. That's because interest builds on itself over time, so even small amounts saved consistently can grow over time. When you plant a seed and watch it grow, the sooner you start, the more you get in the end.

Setting up a savings account or having a piggy bank can be easy ways for teens to start saving. You should save every week, whether it's a portion of your weekly pay or a portion of the money you make from your part-time job.

Simple Investment Options for Teens

Investing may sound like something only adults can do, but there are easy and safe ways for teens to spend their money. When you're young, the point of investing isn't always to make a lot of money but to learn how investments work.

You can get teens to start investing right away with a savings account that makes interest. Even if the returns aren't very high, it's a risk-free method to get started learning how to make money on your money.

For people who want to take their investments a little further, government bonds or mutual funds made for young buyers can be good places to start. These choices let you get into investing with less danger, so they're good for people who are just starting out.

Studying the stock market via computer games or apps made for learning is another fun way to get started. You can use these sites to spend fake money in real stocks to get real-world experience without risking any real money.

Financial Goals and Planning

When it comes to managing your finances, setting financial goals is a crucial step. These goals provide purpose and direction to your financial endeavors, whether they are short-term goals, such as saving for a new gadget, or long-term goals, like preparing for university.

Clarity and realism are key when setting financial goals. Instead of a vague goal like "save money for college," it's more effective to define a specific goal such as "save

$500 by the end of the year." This specificity makes it easier to plan your actions and monitor your progress.

Creating a plan to achieve your goals is an integral part of financial planning. It involves calculating how much you need to save or invest each month and selecting the most suitable methods to reach your objectives.

It's important to remember that financial planning is not a one-time task. It requires regular review and adjustments to align with changing goals and financial circumstances.

In addition to accumulating wealth, saving and investing teach valuable lessons about managing money wisely and understanding its value. For teenagers, learning to save, exploring smart spending habits, and setting clear financial goals pave the way for a secure financial future. It's a journey that starts with small steps and culminates in significant achievements in managing your own finances

Earning More Money

Making more money is an important part of becoming financially independent. Teenagers often start this journey by looking for ways to make money, like part-time work, freelancing, or starting their own businesses. This section aims to show you different ways teens can make money and give tips on balancing work and school duties.

Exploring Part-Time Jobs and Freelancing

Teenagers often get part-time jobs to make extra cash. They not only bring in money but also teach important life lessons like obligations, time management, and the value of money. Depending on your skills and hobbies, you may be able to find work in retail or as a tutor.

In the digital age we live in now, freelancing has also become an open way to make money. Teenagers can find freelance work online if they know how to write, make graphic designs, or build websites. Places like Upwork and Fiverr let freelancers and customers meet and work together. You can work from home as a freelancer and choose your own hours and tasks.

If you're under 18 and want to work part-time or as a freelancer, you should look into the job requirements, payment terms, and any legal issues that might come up. Talk to a parent or guardian about these opportunities to make sure they are safe and legal.

Entrepreneurial Ideas for Teens

There is no set age to become an entrepreneur; it's all about making chances. Teenagers naturally know about innovations and trends, which can be very helpful when they want to start their own businesses. Some easy business ideas are mowing lawns, washing cars, taking care of pets, or selling baked goods or crafts you've made yourself.

Thanks to the growth of social media and online marketing, teen businesses now have many more options. You can become an entrepreneur today by doing things like starting a YouTube channel, handling social media for local businesses, or making your own app.

To make your teen business work, you need to find a need or area of interest and use your skills and imagination to meet it. Being resilient is also crucial because being a business often means making mistakes.

Balancing Work and School

Making money is fun and gives you confidence, but balancing work and school is important. Education should always be a top concern because it sets people up for future success. To keep this balance, here are some tips:

Set priorities and make plans. Use a notebook or an app to keep track of your work and school obligations. Set priorities for your jobs and use your time wisely.

Communicate with Employers. Tell your boss the truth about your school obligations. Most employers are ready to work with students' flexible schedules.

Do what's best for your health. Get enough sleep and eat well. With so many things to do, it's easy to get burned out.

Set goals that are attainable; know your limits. If your job is making it hard for you to do well in school, you may need to cut back on your hours or look for a less stressful job.

If you're feeling too stressed, don't be afraid to talk to your loved ones, teachers, or counsellors. They can give you advice and help.

When we were in middle school, I met Mia. But it wasn't until our junior year of high school that I saw a brighter, more business-minded side of her. Beginning a small business was a fantastic journey for her and an inspiring one for someone my age.

Mia was good at baking all the time. People at school talked about her cookies and cupcakes all the time. While she was talking with other people in the cafeteria one day, Mia brought up an idea which eventually led to her becoming an entrepreneur. She thought, "What if I start selling my baked goods?" "I mean, everyone seems to love them." It was just a thought, but it marked the start of something big.

She began by baking in her home and selling to family and friends. Mia had even bigger plans, though. She made an Instagram account for her business and used catchy titles and appealing photos to show off her tasty treats. There was a huge reaction. A lot of orders came in, not just from kids but also from parents and teachers.

The thing that impressed me the most was how hard Mia worked to balance her business with her schoolwork. She was very good at managing her time; she set aside specific times to do her chores, bake, and relax. Even though it wasn't always easy, Mia was always determined.

Her small business became famous in the area very quickly. A lot of people come to her booth every week at the farmer's market in our town on the weekends. The most important thing to Mia was how much money she made and how she changed as a person. She became more sure of herself and responsible, and I really admired how well she managed her time.

The most exciting thing about Mia's story was how ready she was to change and learn. She taught herself how to market her business, took online classes to get better at baking, and even learned basic accounting to help her handle her money.

Mia started her business because she loved baking. It grew into a successful small business that everyone in our town knew about. Her journey showed how powerful an idea can be when you work hard and have the guts to take a chance. It showed us, her peers, that when it comes to business, age doesn't matter and that we, too, could make our dreams come true with hard work and passion.

"Dream big and dare to fail."

Start Today

- Start today by writing down the things you spend every day. This easy step can help you see how you spend your money and start making a budget that works.

- You might want to open a savings account if you don't already have one.

- Every week, try to learn a new concept about money, like interest rates, budgeting, or the basics of investing. You can do this by using school, online, or book-based tools.

Let's explore personal development and decision-making skills.

Digital Apps for Banking, Saving and Investing

There are many applications for financial budgeting, and most offer a free introduction period, which allows for a trial run.

Copper: is an excellent tool for teenagers to gain financial independence. It empowers teens to manage their money on their own while teaching them smart financial habits.

Toshl: For a straightforward approach to budgeting, check out Toshl. It offers a simple interface to track income, expenses and view financial insights. Toshl simplifies the budgeting process, making it accessible and easy for teenagers to manage their finances. The visualizations and analytical tools provide valuable insights to help teens make better financial decisions.

Greenlight: Want to keep your parents in the loop of your money matters? Family financial planning is easy with Greenlight, the budgeting app designed for parents to team up with their teens. Your family can customize parental controls, add chore lists, set up allowances, and even invest money. Perfect for teenagers whose finances are still tied to their parents and who prefer a collaborative approach to financial responsibility. Greenlight combines budgeting with parental involvement, making it a valuable tool for teens like you to ease into financial responsibility. It's designed with collaboration and guidance in mind while still giving teens control over their own money.

Chapter 4: Decision-Making and Problem Solving

Did you know? An average adult makes about 35,000 remotely conscious decisions each day. It may sound crazy, but researchers at Cornell University have found that every day, we make thousands of decisions, some of which are small and some of which are big. This fact shows how important it is to make choices in our lives.

The "**Art of Making Wise Choices**" is a very important skill, especially for teens whose lives are changing quickly and where each choice can significantly impact their future. It's not enough to just be able to choose between options; you have to really understand what each choice means. It means thinking about how these decisions fit with your long-term goals and personal values, as well as how they might affect your life and the lives of others.

The first step in this process is gathering information and understanding why the choice was made. Making good decisions starts with having enough information. It's not just about facts and numbers, though. Paying attention to your gut and feelings is important, as they can give you useful information. Finding a balance between your emotional urges and your logical thinking is hard.

Thinking about how decisions will affect you in the future is also an important part of making smart choices. It's about having the ability to see what will happen and being ready for it. Knowing what will happen in the future helps you make choices that will be good for you in the short and long term.

Teenagers need to work on this skill more than just being able to make good decisions. They need to build a foundation for a thoughtful, meaningful life. It makes you strong because not all choices will lead to the results you want, and being able to learn from mistakes is an important part of growing. Making smart decisions is a process of becoming more self-aware, responsible, and ready to deal with life's challenges.

Accessing Options

When you need to choose what to study in college, how to spend the weekend, or how to organize your time, it's important to think about all your choices. In this process, you don't just look at the options; you also have to understand what each one means and how it can affect you.

Before you can look at your options, you need to be clear on what choice you need to make. Figure out what the issue or chance is that you're facing and what you want to achieve by making your choice. This makes things clearer, which lets you think more carefully about your choices.

Take as much time as you can to learn about all of your choices once you know what the decision means. Do some research, ask questions, and get help from people you trust. It is said that knowledge is power, and the more you know about your options, the better judgment call you can make. But it's important to tell the difference between information that is useful and information that isn't helpful, which can cause analysis paralysis.

Think about what's good and bad about each choice. Weighing the pros and cons of each option helps you understand how it might affect you. In this step, you'll look at each choice's short- and long-term effects and how they fit with your values, goals, and priorities.

Also, it's important to be aware of and question any ideas or biases that might affect how you make decisions. Biases can change the way you see things and make you miss important parts of each choice. A more objective evaluation is possible if you are aware of these flaws and work to change them.

It's also important to think about the opportunity cost or what you might lose if you choose one choice over another. Knowing what you might be giving up is an important part of making decisions because every choice has a trade-off.

After listing the pros and cons, give yourself some time to think. It can help you take a step back and give yourself some space. It also helps to picture what would happen if you made each choice. Imagine yourself after making each choice. This can help you figure out what you really want and what the best thing to do might be.

Get other people involved in the decision-making process, especially if it will affect them. Talking about things can give you new ideas and views that you hadn't thought of before. Keep in mind, though, that you are the only one who can make the final choice, so it's important to trust your gut and good sense.

Finally, make a backup plan. It's possible for choices to go badly, even if all the facts are known. Having a backup plan gives you a safety net and lowers the risk of making the choice.

Decision-Making Process

The decision-making process is a critical aspect of making sound choices, particularly when significant outcomes are on the line. It encompasses several essential steps, each of which is necessary for arriving at a well-considered decision.

The initial step involves identifying the reason for making a decision. While this may appear straightforward, it's crucial to fully grasp the nature of the problem at hand. Recognizing and articulating the problem constitutes the first phase of any process, whether it involves selecting a career path, addressing a conflict, or making a substantial purchase. This step revolves around acknowledging the need for a decision, understanding the implications of that decision, and assessing its impact on others.

Once the need for a decision is clear, the subsequent step entails gathering information. This involves conducting research and collecting data, which could entail consulting experts or peers, studying relevant materials, or reflecting on past experiences. Striking the right balance between obtaining sufficient information to inform the decision without succumbing to analysis paralysis is crucial.

Following the information-gathering stage, it's time to generate a range of potential options or solutions. This phase emphasizes the importance of creativity and open-mindedness. The goal is to generate ideas and explore different avenues without immediate judgment or dismissal. At this juncture, thinking broadly can foster more innovative solutions and uncover options that may not be immediately apparent.

After generating options, the subsequent step involves a critical evaluation of these possibilities. This entails weighing the pros and cons of each option. Consideration should be given to potential outcomes, risks, benefits, alignment with values and goals, and impact on others. This stage demands careful deliberation, as it involves balancing a multitude of factors, such as feasibility, desirability, and utility.

Following the evaluation, the next step is making a choice. This entails selecting the option that, based on the assessment, appears to be the most suitable. While decisiveness is important at this stage, it's essential to acknowledge that most decisions are not black and white and may necessitate compromise or entail some level of risk.

Lastly, reflecting on the process and the choice made is a valuable post-decision step. Reflection allows for an examination of how well the decision-making process functioned and what lessons can be gleaned from the experience. It involves assessing what worked, what could have been done differently, and how the process can be improved for future decisions. This reflective practice is instrumental in personal growth and enhancement in decision-making capabilities over time.

In summary, the decision-making process is a structured series of steps that involves identifying the need for a decision, gathering information, generating options, evaluating those options, making a choice, and engaging in post-decision reflection. This systematic approach facilitates informed and intelligent decision-making, serving as a crucial skill in both personal and professional contexts.

"It's not hard to make decisions when you know what your values are." Roy Disney

Problem-Solving Strategies

Solving problems is important for dealing with simple and complicated problems. It means finding a problem, figuring out what caused it, and fixing it in a good way. Even though problems are very different, using a set of techniques can help you deal with them in a structured way.

The first step in solving a problem is correctly naming and describing it. This may seem simple, but problems are often misidentified or misunderstood, which means that answers don't work. Take the time to figure out the real problem by separating the signs from it. This clarity is very important for handling problems well.

After clarifying the problem, the next step is gathering information and looking at what's going on. To do this, you need to look at the problem from different points of view, understand its context, and think about any important data or history. Having a full picture of the problem is important because it can help you come up with better answers.

Once you understand the problem, the next step is to come up with possible answers. This is where coming up with new ideas and creative thoughts come in handy. Encourage divergent thought, which means looking at more than one idea without judging them right away. Being open to different ways of doing things is important because sometimes the best answer is not the one that seems obvious.

The next step is to evaluate the answers that were made. Believe in their ability to happen and the effects they might have. It is important to consider each option's pros and cons and how they fit with the general rules and goals of the situation. With this review, the choices are narrowed down to the best ones.

After picking an answer, the next step is to put it into action. This means making a plan for how the answer will be used, listing any resources that will be needed, and setting a date for when it will be put into action. As important as the answer is how well it is carried out, planning and management are very important.

After putting the answer into action, it's important to keep an eye on the results and judge how well it worked. This means making sure the problem is still there and knowing how the answer will affect things. If the problem keeps happening or new ones arise, you might have to fix it again and consider other options.

Lastly, it's important to think about how you solved the problem to learn and improve. Think about what went well, what went wrong, and how the process could be improved for next time. Thinking about things helps you solve problems better and gets you ready for new tasks.

To sum up, problem-solving is a multi-step process that includes figuring out what the problem is, coming up with and reviewing possible solutions, putting the chosen solution into action, keeping an eye on the results, and thinking about the process. Following these tips will help you deal with issues more effectively and improve your ability to handle challenges.

Resilience and Coping Mechanisms

Resilience, in essence, is the ability to bounce back after facing failure or adversity. This skill is invaluable, particularly during challenging and stressful times. Developing a toolkit of coping strategies to manage and recover from life's hardships is the essence of building resilience.

A positive mindset serves as the cornerstone of resilience. Viewing problems not as insurmountable obstacles but as challenges to be tackled is a key component of this mindset. Such thinking fosters optimism and positivity even in the face of adversity. It involves letting go of the things beyond your control and focusing on what you can influence.

Cultivating a robust support network is another critical facet of resilience-building. Having individuals you can rely on for emotional support, guidance, and assistance makes a significant difference. These supportive figures could be close friends, mentors, or even professional counselors. They provide a listening ear for your concerns and offer the much-needed backing during tough times.

Self-care is an integral component of resilience. This entails looking after both your physical and mental well-being. Prioritizing regular exercise, a balanced diet, and adequate sleep is crucial. Practices like meditation, yoga, or engaging in activities you enjoy help you relax and clear your mind.

Enhancing problem-solving skills is also pivotal in building resilience. It involves a systematic approach to breaking down problems into manageable components and devising practical solutions. This skill empowers you to take charge and confront challenges with confidence.

Adaptability is yet another vital aspect of stress management. Being flexible and open to change enables you to navigate new situations and discover innovative ways to surmount obstacles. Embracing change as a natural part of life and learning to adapt effectively are integral aspects of adaptability.

Reflecting on past experiences is an important component of resilience-building. Analyzing how you coped with past challenges and the lessons learned from them equips you to face future problems with greater assurance.

Furthermore, retaining a sense of humor can be a powerful resilience tool. Finding humor in yourself and life's quirks can boost your spirits and provide a more balanced perspective on circumstances.

I vividly recall a significant moment during my junior year of high school, which showcased my aptitude for making crucial decisions and effectively tackling challenging problems. At that time, I was an active member of our school's robotics team, and we were gearing up for a major competition that we had been diligently preparing for. However, just a week before the event, our meticulously crafted robot abruptly malfunctioned, casting a shadow of uncertainty over months of dedicated work. It was during this testing moment that I had the opportunity to demonstrate my leadership and problem-solving skills.

As the news of our robot's malfunction sent ripples of concern through the team, I recognized the gravity of the situation. Despite the initial shock, I remained remarkably composed, ready to take charge. Leadership had always been a quality I prided myself on, and this was a moment where it truly came to the forefront.

Without hesitation, I assembled my team, fostering an atmosphere of unity and collective problem-solving. I firmly believed in the power of teamwork and collaboration, especially in the face of adversity. To kickstart our efforts, I organized a brainstorming session, encouraging every team member to contribute their ideas for resolving the issue. This collaborative approach not only eased the tension but also provided a wealth of potential solutions.

What stood out most during this challenging period was my ability to transform what could have been a chaotic and stressful situation into a well-structured problem-solving meeting. With a strategic mindset, I led the team in categorizing the proposed solutions based on their feasibility and potential impact. This step demonstrated my knack for organized thinking and efficient decision-making.

To expedite our troubleshooting process and ensure that no stone was left unturned, I divided the team into smaller groups, each tasked with testing a different proposed solution. This approach not only sped up the diagnostic process but also ensured a comprehensive examination of all potential fixes. My decisiveness and adept decision-making abilities were especially critical during these moments of intense pressure.

Ultimately, we pinpointed the root cause of the issue—an elusive broken wire component. Under my guidance, *the team worked tirelessly to rectify the problem, racing against the clock. While the technical repair was undoubtedly vital, what truly shone through was my capacity to make quick, informed decisions under duress, all while maintaining composure and determination.*

On the day of the competition, our robot performed flawlessly, securing a well-deserved victory for our team. This experience not only solidified our success but also provided an invaluable learning opportunity for all of us. It was a testament to my ability to lead, think critically, and solve complex problems even in the most challenging circumstances.

Start Today

- Pick a small decision that you've been delaying and make it today. It could be what to eat for dinner or which novel to read next.
- Choose a small problem you face every day and find a new way to solve it.
- When you're not sure what to do next, ask a friend or family member what they think to get a different point of view.

Now, we'll focus on communication skills, vital for personal and professional relationships

Chapter 5: Effective Communication Skills

"Effective communication is the bridge between confusion and clarity."

Nat Turner

Did you know? Studies, including one by Mehrabian and Ferris, show that only 7% of communication is verbal?" The rest is non-verbal (55%) and tone of voice (38%). This shocking number shows how important it is to not only say what we mean but also say it correctly.

Key to Positive Relationships emphasizes how important it is to talk to people in order to build and keep healthy relationships. Sharing information isn't the only thing that makes conversation good; it's also about getting to know someone better. It requires paying attention, knowing, expressing clearly what you think and feel, and picking up on nonverbal cues. By getting good at these things, people can build stronger, better relationships in their personal and work lives. Conflicts can be solved, shared understanding can grow, and a supportive and respectful environment can be created through good communication. Because it's the basis for trust and connection, it's a very important part of building and keeping good partnerships.

We'll learn about Effective Communication Skills in this chapter. These skills are very important for your personal and business success. Communication is more than just giving and receiving knowledge. It's also about figuring out how someone feels and what they're trying to say. Clear communication can help settle disagreements, build trust and respect, and make spaces where love, creativity, and problem-solving can grow.

You can learn how to communicate clearly and get better at it over time. It's about being aware of how we talk to each other and changing it when necessary to make sure conversations are clear, polite, and useful. You'll be able to explain yourself better and understand others by the end of this chapter. This will help you make stronger connections and work together more effectively.

Active Listening and Empathy

Effective communication is a skill that relies heavily on active listening and empathy, two interrelated components that foster understanding, trust, and the establishment of meaningful relationships in both personal and professional interactions.

Active listening transcends the mere act of hearing words. It encompasses a deeper level of engagement, involving undivided attention, comprehension, thoughtful responses, and retention of the information conveyed. Demonstrating full attentiveness communicates to the speaker that their words hold significance for you. Engaging your ears, eyes, and heart is essential for active listening. Nonverbal cues such as nodding, maintaining eye contact, and displaying appropriate facial expressions play a pivotal role in conveying your engagement. Furthermore, active listening involves providing feedback, whether by summarizing key points or seeking clarifications through questions. This not only reassures the speaker that they are being heard but also helps ensure the accurate reception of their message.

In contrast, empathy entails not only understanding but also genuinely feeling the emotions of another person. It requires the ability to step into their shoes and perceive the world from their perspective. When engaging in conversation, empathy involves the recognition and validation of the emotions underlying the speaker's words, even if you may not necessarily share their sentiments. Effective communication with empathy creates a deeper emotional connection, making the speaker feel acknowledged and valued.

The synergy between active listening and empathy results in a potent communication tool. People are more inclined to be open and candid when they believe they are genuinely heard and understood, elevating the quality and significance of interactions. Additionally, conflicts are more likely to find resolution, as a mutual understanding of each other's feelings and viewpoints can lead to more rational and harmonious solutions.

Assertiveness vs. Aggressiveness

It's important to be able to communicate clearly in both your personal and work life. Being able to say what you think, feel, and need is a key part of this skill. However, not every way of communicating is the same. Knowing the key differences between being assertive and aggressive is important to build good relationships and settle disagreements peacefully.

Assertiveness:

When you're assertive, you talk about your thoughts, feelings, wants, and boundaries in a clear and respectful way. It means confidently stating your opinions while still being open to comments and other points of view. People who are assertive know how to stand up for themselves without violating other people's rights or limits.

The practice of clear and straight speech is one of the most important parts of assertive communication. People who are assertive don't use vague or passive words that could cause confusion. They are experts at making their wants, views, and expectations clear and understandable.

Respecting other people is another thing that makes someone bold. When you talk to someone in this way, you don't attack, blame, or put down their feelings. Instead, it respects other people's rights and feelings and tries to keep a polite tone throughout the talk.

Another important part of being confident is actively listening. People who are assertive not only say what they want to say but they also pay close attention to how others respond. While talking to someone, they listen with empathy, showing that they value and accept their point of view.

Also, being assertive is often geared toward fixing problems. People who are assertive don't just want to make their point; and they also want to find answers or compromises that work for everyone. They deal with disagreements in a positive way, trying to find answers instead of arguments.

Lastly, being assertive means knowing how to set and stick to personal limits. People who are assertive are good at setting and sticking to their limits, and they make it clear when someone asks them to do something that goes against their wants or limits.

Aggressiveness

Conversely, aggression is a way of talking marked by being pushy, dominant, and not caring about other people's feelings or limits. People who are aggressive may try to say what they want and need, but they do it in a way that is often hostile, rude, and scary.

Being aggressive is often shown by anger and conflict. People who are aggressive in their communication tend to use hostile and confrontational words, which can make problems worse and make the environment hostile. When people are angry, they often yell, insult, and threaten each other.

Someone who is aggressive also doesn't care about or understand how other people feel. When someone talks aggressively, they only think about their own wants and needs, which often comes at the price of other people's health. When people are violent, they usually don't show empathy or understanding.

Also, being aggressive often means taking over talks and talking over other people. Aggressive speakers might not care about other points of view and take over conversations. This stops proper conversation and shuts down other people's points of view.

Being defensive is another trait that many pushy people share. People who are aggressive are quick to defend themselves when their ideas are questioned. They might get angry when someone criticizes or disagrees with them, which would make things even worse.

Relationships can suffer when someone is aggressive. It can hurt or strain relationships, often leading to disagreements and anger. When someone is being aggressive, they may feel ignored, unheard, and unimportant.

Finding the Right Balance:

Finding the right mix between being assertive and being aggressive is often key to good communication. Aiming for assertive conversation helps people get along, works better when everyone works together and solves problems more quickly.

Being aware of yourself is a key way to find this balance. Figuring out how you talk to people is the first thing that you can do to get better at it. If you tend to be passive or aggressive, make an effort to be more outspoken. Saying "I" words will help you be clear and polite about your feelings and needs. It's important to learn how to say what you're thinking and feeling clearly and straight while still being open to other people's points of view.

Active listening is a fundamental skill that goes well with being forceful. To improve your active listening skills, pay close attention to what other people say, show understanding, and have a productive conversation. This not only shows that you respect other people, but it also helps you see things from their point of view.

Finding the right mix is also very much about having empathy. Even if you don't agree with someone, try to understand how they feel and what they think. Empathy can help people get along and understand each other better, leading to better and more respectful conversations.

In conclusion, learning how to communicate assertively without being hostile is helpful. It helps people get along, works better when everyone works together and solves problems better. We can improve our relationships and get better results in many areas of our lives by learning the differences between these communication styles and practicing being assertive.

Nonverbal Communication

A complex and important part of interaction with others is nonverbal communication. Often called "unspoken language," it's made up of a lot of different cues that people use to communicate without using words or writing. Understanding and using nonverbal communication well can make connecting with others a lot easier, figuring out what's going on, and having good relationships.

Body Language

Body language is one of the most obvious ways that people talk without words. Much information can be communicated through how people move, stand, and make motions. For example, keeping your back straight, looking someone in the eye, and using the right-hand movements can show that you are confident, open, and interested in the conversation. On the other hand, actions like crossing your arms, preventing eye contact, or fidgeting may show that you are protective, uncomfortable, or not interested. Body language is a strong way to show how you feel, what you want, and how you feel about something.

Facial Expressions

The face shows how we feel, and expressions on the face are a way for everyone to communicate their thoughts. For example, a smile shows you are friendly and warm, while a furrowed face can show you are worried or confused. People's facial movements show right away how they're feeling and how they're reacting to something. Understanding other people's facial expressions and showing how you feel through your reactions are important parts of nonverbal communication.

Gestures

Hand moves, nods, and other physical actions are very important for communicating without words. They go along with spoken words and can show agreement, disagreement, stress, or a need for attention. For instance, putting your thumb up means you agree, while putting your finger to your lips means you need to be quiet. But gestures can mean different things in different countries, so it's important to know what they mean when you're talking to people from different backgrounds.

Tone of Voice

The tone of voice, which includes pitch, phrasing, and tone, greatly affects how people understand what people say. A happy, melodic tone can make an assertion sound friendly, while a serious or agitated tone can show anger or a need to act quickly. Mastering the subtleties of tone of voice is important for making sure that messages are received with the right emotional tone and that the feelings behind the words match them.

Eye Contact

Making eye contact is a powerful way to communicate without words that can send many messages. Making and keeping eye contact during a talk shows that you are paying attention and are sincere. But different cultures have different rules about how long and how hard it is to look someone in the eyes, and it's important to be aware of these differences. Long-term eye contact can be seen as a sign of trust and confidence in some cultures but as an act of conflict in others.

Proxemics

Proper use of personal space, or proxemics, is another type of nonverbal interaction. People's distance from others in different social situations shows how comfortable they are with them and what they want to do. For instance, standing close to someone can mean closeness or a sense of urgency, while staying farther away shows care for personal space. In order to get along with other people, you need to understand and accept proxemic cues.

Using nonverbal cues in conversation can either support what is being said or go against it. When lined up, they support what is being said and clarify the point. Inconsistency between spoken and unspoken cues can cause confusion and misunderstanding, which shows how important it is for communication to be consistent.

Additionally, non-verbal communication is very helpful for figuring out how someone feels and wants, especially when words are limited. It lets people pick up on small clues that aren't always said out loud. For example, if a co-worker is uncomfortable with a plan, their face may show it, even if they don't say anything.

Conflict Resolution for Teens

Conflict is an inevitable aspect of human interaction, and it tends to arise more frequently during the teenage years as individuals navigate the challenges of gaining independence. It is crucial for teenagers to acquire conflict resolution skills to address issues, disputes, and challenges in a productive and constructive manner.

Active listening serves as the foundational step in resolving disagreements. Teenagers should learn the art of attentive listening to others' concerns and viewpoints without interrupting or prematurely forming judgments.

Active listening entails maintaining eye contact, nodding to convey understanding, and paraphrasing what the other person has expressed to ensure clarity. By demonstrating respect for the other person's perspective, teens can establish a solid groundwork for conflict resolution.

Understanding and expressing feelings are pivotal aspects of problem-solving. Teenagers should become adept at recognizing their own desires and emotions and articulating them assertively and clearly. Teens can communicate their feelings without resorting to criticism or blame by employing "I" statements such as "I feel upset when..." or "I require..." Similarly, comprehending the emotions of the other party is crucial for empathetic communication.

Engaging in rude and angry exchanges exacerbates conflicts. Teens should be encouraged to maintain composure and politeness, even when addressing sensitive subjects. It is of utmost importance to refrain from name-calling, shouting, or launching personal attacks during conflict resolution attempts. Emphasize the significance of addressing the underlying problem rather than making it a personal matter.

Seeking common ground and shared objectives is a valuable strategy for conflict resolution. Teenagers should identify areas where their interests align with those of others and strive to find solutions that enable everyone to achieve their goals. This approach can alleviate tension and promote cooperation.

Teenagers may encounter situations where they are unable to independently resolve complex or distressing issues. It is essential for them to recognize when to seek adult assistance in such circumstances. Trusted adults, such as parents, teachers, or counselors, can assist teenagers in working through their problems and provide valuable guidance.

However, resolving a problem is not the sole objective; it is equally important to forgive and move forward. Teenagers should understand the significance of letting go of anger and negative emotions once a conflict is resolved. Harbouring resentful thoughts can detrimentally impact relationships and hinder personal growth.

Conflict management is a skill that improves with practice. Encourage teenagers to apply these conflict resolution techniques in various aspects of their lives, whether they are dealing with friends, family members, or classmates. The more they utilize these skills, the more confident they will become in effectively addressing disputes.

Teenagers who employ these conflict resolution techniques are better equipped to navigate disagreements, strengthen relationships, and acquire vital life skills. Teaching teenagers how to manage conflicts through empathy, active listening, and a problem-solving mindset prepares them to tackle challenges in a healthy manner, laying the foundation for a lifetime of positive interactions with others.

Building Healthy Friendships

Building and maintaining friendships during your teenage years is of utmost importance as these connections have the potential to last a lifetime. Healthy friendships offer support, companionship, and a profound sense of connection, but they require effort and mutual understanding to flourish.

Respect serves as the cornerstone of any strong friendship. Teenagers should treat their friends with affection and consideration, recognizing their unique value and significance. This entails acknowledging each other's boundaries, actively listening to their perspectives, and refraining from engaging in disrespectful behavior or speech.

Effective communication is vital for the success of any friendship. Teenagers should strive to be open, honest, and attentive in their conversations. Sharing feelings, thoughts, and experiences fosters trust and deepens mutual understanding. Encourage teenagers to discuss their concerns or mistakes rather than allowing them to fester.

Trust is the bedrock of a resilient friendship. Teenagers should aim to be reliable friends who uphold their promises and respect confidences. Loyalty also plays a pivotal role in nurturing healthy friendships. Through both the good times and the bad, friends should offer unwavering support and solidarity.

Shared interests and activities often form the glue that binds friends together. Encourage teenagers to pursue their passions and hobbies, as common interests provide opportunities for quality time spent together.

Empathy and understanding are crucial elements of any thriving friendship. Teenagers should strive to see the world from their friends' perspectives and offer a listening ear during challenging moments. Simple acts of kindness and a willingness to lend support can make a significant difference in a friend's life.

Even in the strongest friendships, disagreements may arise. Teenagers should learn how to navigate conflicts and seek resolution in a constructive manner. Encourage the use of conflict resolution skills, such as active listening and calm communication, to address issues that may surface.

Teaching teenagers the importance of setting and respecting healthy boundaries is imperative. Whether pertaining to personal space, time commitments, or emotional limits, friends should be aware of each other's boundaries. This practice fosters trust and helps prevent misunderstandings.

Teenagers often encounter peer pressure within their social circles. It is essential for them to be mindful of such influences and make decisions aligned with their values and best interests rather than succumbing to external pressures.

Quality should always take precedence over quantity when it comes to friendships. Teenagers should understand that having a small, close-knit group of friends can be more rewarding and fulfilling than maintaining a large circle of acquaintances.

Awareness of the signs of unhealthy or toxic relationships is vital. Teenagers should be equipped to recognize manipulative, negative, or disrespectful dynamics and know when to distance themselves from such connections, seeking assistance from trusted individuals when necessary.

By imparting these guidelines for fostering healthy friendships, teenagers acquire valuable life skills. During their teenage years, they can cultivate friendships that endure, providing companionship, emotional support, and essential social and emotional skills that will serve them throughout their lives.

Start Today

- Actively listen to others, showing empathy and understanding.
- Be open to feedback and different perspectives.
- Be clear and to the point in your communication. Avoid unnecessary jargon.

Next, we'll tackle the art of setting and achieving meaningful goals.

Review Request: "Life Skills for Teens" by K.R. Heywood

We hope this message finds you well! We know your time is valuable, and we appreciate you considering sharing your thoughts on "Life Skills for Teens: Practical Strategies to

Overcome Self-Doubt & Build Self-Esteem, Boost Test Scores and Kick Start your Game Plan for Extra Money" by K.R. Heywood.

Why Your Review Matters

"Life Skills for Teens" is more than just a book; it's a roadmap to personal development, academic excellence, and financial responsibility for teenagers. Your review can help others discover the empowering content within these pages and guide them on their journey through the challenges and triumphs of adolescence.

How to Share Your Thoughts:

- Visit the Book's Page: Go to the book's page on your preferred platform (Amazon, Goodreads, etc.).

- Compose Your Review: Share what you loved about the book, whether it's the practical strategies, the relatable tone, or the valuable life skills covered.

- Rate the Book: Give it a star rating that reflects your overall impression.

Chapter 6: Setting and Achieving Goals

"You should set goals beyond your reach so you always have something to live for." Ted Turner.

Transforming dreams into reality is not just about having a big vision; you also need to make a strategy on how to make that vision turn into desired results. Setting clear, attainable goals and making a step-by-step plan to reach them are part of this. The big dream needs to be broken up into smaller, more doable pieces that can be worked on one at a time.

But taking action isn't enough on its own. Persistence and toughness are very important. From a dream to a reality, the path is often rocky and full of mistakes and failures. Success comes from keeping going, learning from your mistakes, and changing your plans as needed.

You also need to have a lot of faith in yourself and your dream to go through this process. There will always be people who don't believe in you or your abilities, but staying true to your vision and trusting yourself is important for progress.

Vision, action, persistence, and self-belief are the main things that make dreams come true. It's not enough to imagine what it could be; you must work hard and stay determined to make it happen. That's what it means to turn the vague into the real, to make what seemed impossible a normal part of your life.

Welcome to Chapter 7, where we'll talk about how to set and reach your goals. Goals are like a guide in life; they help us know where to go and what to do. Today, we'll talk about why goals are important, how to make them, and the best ways to reach them. Never forget that a trip of a thousand miles starts with one step. Let's go!

Defining S.M.A.R.T. Goals

Starting to set goals is like setting sail on a vast ocean. You need a compass to help you find your way on this trip. It will keep you on track. This is where S.M.A.R.T. goals come in handy. To make an acronym, you need to write down the words "Specific, Measurable, Achievable, Relevant, and Time-bound." Every part of an S.M.A.R.T. goal helps make the aim clear and attainable. Let's look at each part separately to see how they work together to make a strong base for setting goals.

Specific

To make an S.M.A.R.T. plan, you must first be clear about what you want to achieve. You can see exactly what you want to accomplish with specific goals. This understanding helps people focus their efforts and resources in the best way possible. "Get better at math" is not a very specific goal. A more specific goal would be "to raise my math grade from a B to an A by the end of the semester." This level of detail makes it clear what you want to achieve.

Measurable

You should be able to measure your progress toward a goal. The question "How will I know when the goal is reached?" is answered by this section. Having goals that can be measured helps you stay motivated because you can see the changes. The change from a B grade to an A in our math case is what can be measured.

Achievable

Goals should be realistic and doable. Even though it's good to set goals that are hard to reach, they should still be doable. Goals are achievable if they are doable, given the time and resources available. Being aware of your boundaries and working within them is important. For example, getting one grade higher in math is hard, but it is possible with hard work and maybe some extra help from a teacher.

Relevant

Importantly, your goal should be connected to important things in your life, like your values, long-term goals, and job aspirations. An important goal changes the course of your life in a meaningful way. For our math goal, it's important if you need a good math grade to get into the college or job you want.

Time-bound

Every goal needs a due date, a time limit that forces you to concentrate and set priorities. Setting goals with due dates keeps your daily chores from getting in the way of your long-term goals. As a deadline for our math goal, the end of the term makes it clear when we need to finish.

Put into action

Having S.M.A.R.T. goals is one thing, but putting them into action is something else. Let's look at a real-life example:

Imagine you are a high school student wanting to get in better shape. One S.M.A.R.T. goal could be, "Within three months, I want to improve my running endurance so that I can run 5 kilometers without stopping."

Specific: It sets out the exact result (running nonstop for 5 kilometers).

Measurable: The distance and time taken to run can be used to track progress.

Achievable: Building up your fitness to run 5 kilometers is a goal that you can reach with regular training.

Relevant: This goal is relevant if you want to get in better shape or maybe get ready for a school sports event.

Time-bound: The three-month period makes a clear due date.

Overcoming Obstacles and Staying Motivated

Sometimes, reaching your goals takes a lot of effort and failure. It's important to know that running into problems is not a sign of failure but a normal part of the way to success. Getting past these problems requires making a strong plan, being able to adjust to new situations, and keeping a persistent, upbeat attitude.

The first thing you must do to deal with problems is recognize and understand them. Challenges can come from the outside, like not having enough time or resources, or from the inside, like having doubts about yourself or not being motivated. You can make good plans once you know what these problems are. For example, if putting things off is stopping you, you need to know why—whether it's fear of failing, too much to do, or not wanting to do it—so you can fix it.

Once you know what the problems are, you need to think about how to solve them. When you think this way, you stop seeing problems as obstacles and start seeing them as challenges that you can beat. This way of doing things encourages creative thought and strategies that focus on finding solutions. These problems can seem less scary if you break them down into smaller, easier-to-handle parts. For example, if you have trouble managing your time, it might help to look at your daily plan and change it so that you have time for your goals.

Another important approach is to look for help and resources. Outside help can give you useful ideas and strategies, like getting advice from a mentor, joining a group of people with similar goals, or using online tools. This network gives valuable advice and keeps people accountable and motivated.

Another important part of getting past problems is staying motivated. It can be very inspiring to celebrate small wins along the way. These celebrations help you feel good about your success, no matter how small, and keep you motivated to reach your goals. This feeling of having done something great is very motivating and helps you keep your mind on the next step in your journey.

When things go wrong, it's also important to be able to adapt and change. Dealing with problems can force you to rethink and change your plans or goals. You can make a big difference on your way to your goals if you are open to change and able to adapt to new situations. This gives you the freedom to stay on track, even if problems come up out of the blue.

Having a positive mood is very important for getting through tough times. Problems can be discouraging, but keeping a cheerful attitude can help you see them in the bigger picture. Being positive makes you stronger, so you can keep going after your goals even if things go wrong. This positive outlook is important for keeping up the energy and drive you need to overcome challenging situations.

Finally, picturing yourself succeeding can be very helpful. Imagine yourself reaching your goals on a regular basis. This can help you stay committed and motivated. This picture will always remind you of your goals and the rewards waiting at your trip's end.

Tracking Progress

Monitoring progress is a fundamental component in the process of attaining one's goals. The significance lies not only in achieving the final objective but also in comprehending and valuing the journey undertaken to reach it. Monitoring one's progress is essential for sustaining motivation, adapting techniques as necessary, and acknowledging accomplishments, regardless of their magnitude.

The significance of monitoring progress is in its capacity to comprehensively depict one's current position in respect to their objective. This mechanism provides a means of assessing one's progress and determining whether adjustments to one's efforts are necessary. For instance, if the objective is to enhance academic performance, consistent monitoring of one's grades and study habits might yield significant insights into progress and areas that need improvement.

An efficacious approach to monitoring development involves the establishment of milestones. These smaller objectives serve as incremental milestones towards the overarching objective. Milestones divide a big objective into smaller, more manageable segments, reducing feelings of overwhelm and increasing the likelihood of successful attainment. As an illustration, in the context of authoring a novel, one's objectives may encompass the accomplishment of many milestones, such as finalizing the plan, completing individual chapters, and subsequently engaging in the process of rewriting and editing the manuscript. Every accomplished milestone represents progress towards the final objective and warrants recognition.

Keeping a development log or diary is an additional beneficial approach. The means of documentation can take the form of either a tangible notebook or a digital platform, wherein one consistently records their endeavors, accomplishments, and introspections. Maintaining a personal journal facilitates retrospective reflection, enabling individuals to gauge their own growth and derive substantial motivation, particularly during periods characterized by sluggish or stagnant advancement.

The utilization of technology and applications can also enhance the efficiency of progress tracking. A wide array of applications exists that have been developed explicitly for the purpose of setting goals and monitoring progress. These tools frequently incorporate functionalities such as reminders, progress bars, and statistics, which streamline and augment the tracking process.

Regular review sessions play a crucial role in the learning process. Allocating regular intervals, whether on a weekly or monthly basis, for the purpose of evaluating one's development aids in maintaining a high level of concentration and dedication. During these meetings, individuals have the opportunity to evaluate the effectiveness of their strategies and identify areas that require modification, allowing for required improvements to be made to their strategy. This occasion also presents a time for introspection regarding one's accomplishments and obstacles, with the aim of deriving valuable insights from both experiences.

The provision of feedback is of utmost importance in the process of monitoring and evaluating development. Seeking feedback from mentors, peers, or professionals can provide external perspectives on your progress. This input possesses significant value in the identification of areas for improvement that the individual may have neglected.

Monitoring progress encompasses more than simply evaluating achievement in relation to the ultimate objective. It is imperative to recognize and value the exertion and development that transpire throughout the course of the endeavor. Acknowledging the acquired abilities, acquired knowledge, and demonstrated resilience is as significant to the attainment of the objective.

The integration of flexibility into the tracking process is crucial. Occasionally, objectives undergo a transformation, or situations undergo modifications, necessitating adaptations to one's strategic blueprint. Maintaining flexibility and adjusting tracking systems in response to these changes is essential for ensuring alignment with current objectives and reality.

In summary, the process of monitoring progress encompasses various aspects, such as establishing significant points of achievement, maintaining a written record, using technological tools, engaging in periodic evaluations, soliciting input from others, recognizing individual development, and demonstrating adaptability. By using a systematic method of monitoring one's development, individuals can enhance their likelihood of attaining their objectives and simultaneously develop a more profound comprehension and admiration for the process of personal and professional advancement. This method transforms the act of creating goals into a dynamic and enriching endeavor, replete with opportunities for learning and self-exploration.

Celebrating Success

Celebrating success is a crucial element in the journey towards achieving your goals. It serves as a means of recognizing and appreciating your hard work and accomplishments, while also providing various other benefits that contribute to your overall growth and motivation.

In the context of your goal pursuit, envision your path as a compelling story where every stage of hard work and persistence leads to a moment of victory. Celebrating these moments of success, whether they mark the culmination of a goal or a significant milestone along the way, is vital. Self-praise is not merely a self-indulgent act; it's a form of reflection on your progress, personal growth, and the lessons learned throughout your journey.

The ways in which you choose to celebrate your success can vary widely and should align with your personal preferences. Some may opt for grand gestures, such as sharing their achievements with family and friends, throwing a party, or enjoying a night out. Others may prefer quieter, more introspective celebrations, such as treating themselves to a special reward, taking a day to relax, or journaling their thoughts. The size of the celebration matters less than the act of acknowledging your success.

Sharing your accomplishments with those who have supported you along the way, whether they are teachers, family members, friends, or colleagues, is another significant aspect of celebrating success. Sharing your triumphs strengthens your relationships, allows others to be a part of your journey, and enables them to share in your joy. Recognizing that they see and appreciate your hard work can be deeply fulfilling and motivating.

Celebrations also serve as powerful psychological cues that reinforce the link between hard work, persistence, and positive outcomes. This positive feedback loop boosts your confidence and enthusiasm for taking on new challenges and pursuing future goals.

Furthermore, celebrations offer an opportunity for reflection. They encourage you to revisit your journey, understand the problems you've overcome, and appreciate the personal growth you've achieved. This reflective process involves asking questions such as "What went well?" and "What could be improved?" and extracting valuable lessons that can be applied to future endeavors.

It's important to note that success doesn't always have to be monumental to warrant celebration. Even small achievements deserve recognition, as they represent steps in the right direction. Celebrating these minor victories keeps you motivated and on track, particularly when working on long-term projects or pursuing distant goals.

Adjusting Your Goals over Time

Making changes to your goals over time is an important part of setting and achieving your goals. That means you know that as we grow and our lives change, so do our goals. They need to change to fit our new hopes and needs. Being able to change helps us keep our goals current, attainable, and important.

Different things can make it necessary to change goals. If your personal hobbies change, you learn something new, your life changes, or you run into an unexpected problem, you may need to reevaluate your goals. You might choose a job path based on an interest, but as time goes on, you may find new interests that take you in a different direction. It's not a sign of failure that things are changing; it's just a normal part of growing and developing as a person.

Thinking about your goals is the first step in changing them. Take some time to think about how your goal has changed since you first made it. Has anything changed about your beliefs or your life? Have you faced problems or had chances that you didn't expect? By thinking about these questions, you can figure out why you might need to make a change and what that change should be.

It is important to keep a balance between reality and ambition when you change your goals. Your goals should still push you and help you grow, but they also need to be attainable. It's not only innovative, but also useful to change your goal to something that you can actually reach if your situation changes. But if you find that a goal is too easy to reach, maybe because of personal growth or outside forces, it's time to set a higher goal.

If you change your goals, you should also look over your plans and methods for achieving them. When your goals change, so should the ways you use to reach them. You could learn new things, change your habits, or even switch up your daily routine. Ensuring your actions align with your new goals is very important.

Communication is very important when changing goals, especially involving others. If your goals have to do with work or personal relationships, you should talk about these changes with the right people to get support.

It's also important to welcome the chances to learn that come with changing your goals. When you look at your goals again and change them, you learn more about what works and what doesn't and how your wants and needs change over time. This method of learning is beneficial because it helps you become more self-aware and better at making decisions.

Finally, keep in mind that changing your goals is an ongoing process, not something that happens just once. Reviewing and changing your goals on a regular basis will help them stay in line with who you are and what you want to achieve as life goes on. Changing your goals all the time keeps them fresh and useful. This makes having goals an active and flexible part of your personal and professional growth.

Start Today

- ➢ Take a quiet hour to look over your current goals. Ask yourself if they still excite you and fit into your life as it is now.
- ➢ Start a simple diary or note on your phone where you track any changes you make to your goals and why.
- ➢ Your goals are yours alone. They should serve you and your happiness, so adjust them as often as you need to maintain that alignment.

Let's dive into understanding emotions and building emotional intelligence.

Serious Help with Goal Setting

Setting Goals and monitoring them is crucial to achieving success. Old school using a notebook following the SMART system will work, but numerous digital apps can help, usually with a free version and some with upgrades.

Goal-tracking apps help individuals and teams set goals and track their progress towards those goals.

Habit tracking tools can send you reminders and notify you whenever your progress isn't going according to schedule.

Your goal-tracking app should also use a workstream to break down your ambitious goals into smaller tasks.

This way, you can work towards your ambitious goals in increments instead of trying to reach them all at once and not getting the best results.

Suggestions:

Click Up: Powerful free version with unlimited users. Easy-to-use user interface with online and offline mode.

Free Forever: $0 Unlimited: $7/month per user

Strides: a flexible goal-setting app that tracks good and bad habits and SMART goals.

Use dashboards to view all your goals and work habits.

Way of Life: a free goal tracker app that helps users build on their goals and break bad habits. The app is well-known for its simplicity and beautiful design. Track any daily goal or routine using the unique color-coded system. There are reminders to keep you on track until a positive habit is formed or a bad habit is broken

Chapter 7: Emotional Intelligence and Self-Awareness

Emotional intelligence has a greater impact on personal and professional success than IQ. Studies have shown that Emotional Intelligence accounts for nearly 90% of what sets high achievers apart from others with similar technical skills and knowledge.

Life is like riding a roller coaster: there are ups and downs, turns and twists. Many times, our feelings change quickly and catch us off guard. Emotional intelligence gives us the tools to deal with our feelings in an intelligent way. It means recognising, understanding, and controlling our own and other people's feelings. We can easily handle life's emotional upheavals, making choices based on logic and a deep understanding of how people think and feel.

Identifying and Managing Emotions

Life requires you to be able to recognize and control your emotions. It's like being a detective and a coach for your own feelings at the same time. A lot can change in your life if you learn how to deal with your feelings in a good way and understand what you're feeling and why.

It's not always hard to figure out how you're feeling. Feelings like happiness, anger, and sadness are clear and easy to spot. On the other hand, feelings aren't always simple or easy to understand. It's like trying to get a knot out of a rope. You could be sad or nervous for no apparent reason. To control your feelings, you must first take a moment to think and feel. Be honest with yourself about how you feel and why you think you feel that way. This easy act of thinking about things can be constructive.

Also, our bodies can tell a lot about how we're feeling. Having a beating heart when you're stressed or a heavy feeling in your chest, when you're sad, can help you figure out how you're feeling. Paying attention to these physical emotions can help you understand how you're feeling.

The next step after figuring out what you're feeling is figuring out why you feel that way. Sometimes, the reasons are clear, like being pleased with a good grade or angry over an argument with a friend. At other times, it's not so clear why. You might need to dig deeper to get to the bottom of how you feel. This could mean thinking about recent events, things that are stressing you out right now, or even things that happened in the past that are still affecting how you feel now.

Managing your feelings is very important after you have identified and understood them. It doesn't mean hiding or ignoring how you feel. It's about recognizing and finding good ways to talk about and deal with them. A good way to deal with your thoughts is to tell someone you trust about them. Talking about what you're going through can help you feel better and give you new ways to look at your situation.

Writing is another great way to deal with your feelings. Writing down your thoughts and feelings in a book can help you deal with them and find relief. There's no one else around, so you can be fully honest and unfiltered, which can be very healing.

Deep breathing and other simple methods can also work amazingly well. When you're feeling too emotional, taking a few slow, deep breaths can help calm you down and clear your mind, making it easier to deal with how you're feeling.

Finding an exercise that helps you deal with your feelings can also be helpful. This could be doing something active like running or playing a sport, something creative like drawing or making music, or something relaxing like yoga or meditation. These things give you a healthy way to deal with your feelings and help you take your mind off bad feelings.

Last but not least, it's important to be able to control your feelings and think things through before acting. Emotions can make you act without thinking, which you may later regret. It can save you a lot of trouble and regret if you take a moment to think about how to react best.

Controlling your feelings means being aware of them, recognizing them, and reacting to them in a healthy and helpful way. Mastering this skill takes time, patience, and kindness toward oneself, but it can improve your mental health, make your connections stronger, and make your life more fulfilling in general.

Building Resilience

Building resilience is a bit like preparing for a long hike. You know that the path won't always be smooth; there may be steep hills and rough ground, but you also know that you can make it through and enjoy the ride if you think about it the right way.

Being emotionally strong enough to get back on your feet after a bad experience is a necessary trait to have. Think of a time when you had to deal with something really tough, like failing a test or getting into a big fight with a friend. Being angry or let down is normal, but being strong helps you overcome these feelings and move on. Like having a strength inside you, that helps you get through hard times.

Getting used to problems and failures is the first thing that you need to do to become more resilient. Everyone has them. You can't avoid these problems; you have to learn how to deal with them. You don't always win at games; learn from your mistakes and try again. Life is the same. It's okay when things are unplanned; they can teach you a lot.

A big part of being resilient is having good relationships with other people. While you're having a rough time, it can really help to talk to people you trust. They could be your family, friends, teacher, or coach. Feel free to talk to these people, get help, or just listen when you need to. It's like having a group cheering you on and helping you when you fall.

Taking care of yourself is also important for getting stronger. In other words, take care of your mind and body. Some important things to do are eat well, get enough sleep, and work out. They help your body stay strong and ready for stress. It's not just about health, though. Doing things you enjoy, like sports or hanging out with friends, is good for your mental health. Feeling good in body and mind makes it easier to deal with the problems that come up in life.

Finding the good in bad situations can also help you get stronger. It's not about ignoring the bad things; it's about getting the big picture. Maybe a mistake taught you something important or showed you how strong you really are. These good things won't make the bad times go away, but they can help you see things in a new way and give you something to hold on to.

Last but not least, being strong means knowing when to get help. Sometimes, things get too hard to handle by yourself, and that's fine. That you need help is not a sign of weakness; it's an intelligent thing to do. Finding the help you need, like talking to a counselor, asking a teacher for extra help, or calling a family member, is a big part of being strong.

Building resilience means knowing that problems will come up and that you have the power to deal with them. It's about taking care of yourself, staying in touch with people, looking for the good in bad situations, and not being afraid to ask for help when you need it. You don't just get through hard times when you're resilient; you grow and get better because of them.

Self-Reflection and Self-Regulation

Self-reflection and self-regulation are two important parts of emotional intelligence that work hand-in-hand to help us understand and control our inner lives. When we take a step back and look at our thoughts, feelings, and actions, we are self-reflecting. It's kind of like having a deep talk with yourself. As part of this process, we ask ourselves why we feel the way we do, what makes us feel a certain way, and how our responses to these feelings fit with our values and goals. For example, self-reflection after a fight would include thinking about what emotions were at play, why the fight happened, and how our reaction to it affected the situation.

Conversely, self-regulation controls how we react to our feelings and the new ideas we get from thinking about ourselves. It means controlling our urges and feelings and acting carefully and measuredly when things happen. Having this skill is very helpful when you are feeling stressed or upset. For instance, if we realize through self-reflection that we get angry in high-stress situations, then self-regulation would mean noticing this pattern and trying to react more calmly in the future.

To improve these skills, you must be patient and keep practicing. Setting aside time to think about yourself regularly is often the first step. This could be done by meditating, writing in a diary, or just being still and thinking. The important thing is to make a place where we can talk about our feelings and thoughts in an open and honest way. This helps us learn more about ourselves, like our weaknesses, skills, and things that make us feel bad.

At the same time, building self-regulation means coming up with ways to control our emotions. This could mean doing things like breathing exercises, practicing awareness, or even asking other people for feedback on our behavior to see it from their point of view. It means being able to tell when our emotions are getting out of hand and using skills to stay calm and logical.

We can't say enough how important it is to think about and control our behavior. These skills help us deal with the problems we face in life better. We can improve how we interact with others, make better choices, and stay calm inside even when things are going badly if we understand and learn to control our emotions.

Also, as we get better at self-reflection and self-control, we get better at understanding how other people feel. Knowing how we feel helps us understand how others feel, leading to deeper connections and more meaningful interactions.

In the end, self-reflection and self-control are very important for mental health and personal growth. As a result, they help us understand how our brains and hearts work and give us the tools to get through tough emotional situations. As we keep working on these skills, we learn more about ourselves and get better at living a healthy and satisfying life.

Empathy towards Others

Understanding and caring about other people is an important part of emotional intelligence. It helps us connect with the people around us. It means understanding and sharing someone else's thoughts, seeing things from their point of view, and feeling their emotions as if they were your own. Empathy is more than just recognizing how someone else feels; it means really feeling what they feel and letting that knowledge shape how you connect with them.

Try putting yourself in someone else's shoes and feeling their joys, fears, happiness, and pain. This is what it looks like to care. Being able to deeply understand someone emotionally goes beyond just feeling sorry for them; it means feeling with them. For example, when a friend is having a hard time, empathy means not only noticing their sadness but also feeling what they're feeling, seeing things from their point of view, and giving them support that fits with how they feel.

Listening and observing are the first steps in developing understanding. It means really focusing on what other people are saying, both what they say and how they say it. It means listening not just to answer but also to really understand. This means giving attention to what they say, how they speak, how they move, and how they look. It means being in the talk, giving the other person your full attention, and recognizing how they feel without giving them advice or solutions right away.

Being empathetic changes relationships in big ways. People feel seen, heard, and understood, which builds trust and leads to deeper relationships. When there is a disagreement, empathy can help settle it because it helps you see things from the other person's point of view, which leads to more caring and effective problem-solving.

Also, understanding isn't just for close friends and family. There are bigger social settings where it's very important, like jobs, schools, and communities. It encourages people from different backgrounds to be tolerant, understand each other, and work together. We can help make the world a more caring and understanding place by practicing empathy.

"He who smiles rather than rages is always the stronger."

Conflict Resolution

The role of emotional intelligence in conflict resolution cannot be overstated, as it provides a structured and effective approach to managing and resolving differences through understanding and empathy. Here's an in-depth exploration of the various facets of emotional intelligence in conflict resolution:

Self-Awareness:

Self-awareness is the foundational step in emotional intelligence for conflict resolution. It involves recognizing and understanding your own emotional responses to a problem. This self-awareness allows individuals to approach conflicts with a rational mindset rather than being driven by intense emotions like anger or irritation. By cultivating self-awareness of one's emotional state, individuals can better regulate their reactions and adopt a more constructive attitude when faced with conflicts.

Empathy:

Empathy is a critical component of emotional intelligence in conflict resolution. It involves making an effort to understand the situation from the other person's perspective. Empathy doesn't necessarily mean agreeing with their viewpoints; it means recognizing and validating the emotions and ideas expressed by others. Empathy deepens the understanding of the dispute at hand and can help identify common ground. Active listening, a core component of effective communication, plays a significant role in empathy as it involves fully focusing on comprehending and absorbing the information conveyed by the speaker rather than just waiting for an opportunity to respond.

Self-Regulation:

Self-regulation is another vital aspect of emotional intelligence. It pertains to the ability to manage impulsive behaviors and responses during conflicts. For instance, individuals might feel a strong urge to react with anger when they perceive themselves under attack. Emotional intelligence encourages individuals to pause, engage in emotional self-regulation, and then formulate a composed and rational response. Self-regulation ensures that responses are more likely to lead to favorable outcomes rather than escalating conflicts.

Effective Communication:

Effective communication is the linchpin of conflict resolution. It involves articulating one's emotions and viewpoints clearly and courteously, while refraining from making accusatory statements or exacerbating the situation. Active listening is also crucial to ensure that the opposing party feels heard and understood. Effective communication helps mitigate misunderstandings and facilitates the resolution of underlying conflicts.

Collaborative Approach:

Emotional intelligence promotes a collaborative approach to conflict resolution. Rather than viewing conflicts as contests with winners and losers, they are seen as collaborative efforts to find mutually agreeable solutions. This approach involves identifying the underlying factors contributing to the dispute and then working together to discover resolutions that satisfy all parties involved. It shifts the focus from a combative standpoint to one characterized by collaboration and mutual respect.

Strategic Disengagement:

Emotional intelligence also recognizes the importance of identifying instances where emotions have escalated to a level that hinders constructive dialogue. In such cases, adopting a strategic approach may involve temporarily disengaging from the discourse, allowing all participants to regain their composure before resuming the conversation.

Emotional intelligence provides a robust set of skills that can be harnessed to effectively address conflicts while upholding respect, empathy, and efficiency. This approach fosters a deeper understanding of all perspectives involved in a conflict, paving the way for resolutions that not only restore harmony but also support individual and interpersonal growth. Through emotional intelligence, which encompasses understanding and regulating emotions, empathetic listening, and collaborative problem-solving, conflicts can transform into opportunities for strengthening relationships and fostering improved understanding.

Start Today

- Pick one aspect of emotional intelligence, like empathy or self-regulation, and focus on improving it in your daily life.

- Find a local or online group focused on personal development or emotional intelligence. Sharing experiences with others can be incredibly valuable.

- Spend a few minutes each night thinking about your emotional responses throughout the day. Consider what you did well and what you could improve.

I've had trouble understanding and controlling my feelings for as long as I can remember. It was like being on a boat in a rough sea: you could feel every wave and gust of wind, but you had no idea how to get through it. This caused a lot of problems, mainly with my family and close friends. Then something changed.

It all began with a big fight between my best friend Alex and me. We were going on a trip over the weekend but couldn't decide where to go. He liked the beach more than the mountains. Things got heated very quickly, and I didn't know it when we were both yelling. Even though I was very angry and upset, I stopped and took a deep breath. It was a small thing I did, but it helped me calm down after feeling so upset.

I knew this wasn't just about the trip during that short break. I was angry that I always felt like other people's wants and needs came before mine. I could tell Alex felt the same way. This was a time to think about myself, and it helped me see the bigger problem.

I chose to do something different and try to see things from Alex's point of view. "I understand you're really looking forward to relaxing by the beach," I said. "I've been ignoring that because I've been so caught up in my own wants." Saying this not only eased the stress but it also helped Alex talk about how he felt.

As soon as we both said what we were thinking and feeling, the argument turned into a useful talk. We came to understand that our friendship was more important than where we were going. We planned a trip that would include both the mountains and the beach as a middle ground.

This event changed the way I see things. It showed me how important emotional intelligence is, especially when trying to solve problems. I learned how important it is to know yourself and how being aware of my feelings could keep them from taking over my life. I saw how empathy could turn a fight into a time of getting to know each other and connecting. And most importantly, I knew that the best way to settle a disagreement was to talk things out and be ready to find a middle ground.

I've been more aware of my feelings and behaviors since then. I've been working on it, and it's not just for disagreements. I use it in everyday talks, too. This hasn't just made my relationships better and given me peace of mind and helped me keep my feelings in check.

Getting smarter about emotions is a process that never ends. Sometimes, it's hard, and I fall back into old habits. But every time I handle a tough talk or help calm down a tense situation well, I remember how important it is to understand and control my emotions. It's like learning to sail on that rough sea, and each day, I feel like I can steer the boat better, no matter how rough the water is.

Now, we'll explore how to handle social and peer pressure

Chapter 8: Peer Pressure and Healthy Relationships

Research shows that the brain doesn't fully grow until around age 25. This is especially important for learning about how teens and young adults make choices and deal with peer pressure. The part of the brain that handles making choices and managing risks is still developing during these years. This makes teens and young adults more likely to be influenced by their friends. This exciting fact sets the stage for what we'll talk about in this chapter.

Balancing Peer Influence

Think of yourself as walking on a tightrope. On one side are your choices, and on the other are your friends' views. This is, a lot of the time, how it feels to deal with peer pressure. You have to find a balance between being yourself and getting in with your friends. At some point in their lives, everyone feels the push and pull of group pressure. It could be something as easy as friends pushing you to try a new style or something more complicated like feeling forced to do things that make you feel bad.

But peer pressure isn't always a bad thing. Other times, it can push you to try new things, get better, or leave your comfort zone for the better. You need to be able to tell the difference between good group pressure that helps you grow and bad pressure that pulls you away from who you are or want to be.

You need to know your own standards and limits to deal with peer pressure. Building a strong sense of self is important if you don't want to give in to the push to fit in. This doesn't mean you should turn down every idea or action your friends give you. Instead, you should think carefully about whether their impact fits with your own values and goals.

Recognizing Positive and Negative Peer Pressure

Peer pressure is a formidable force, especially during the teenage years when individuals often grapple with the urge to fit in and be accepted by their peers. Learning to handle this pressure is not just a valuable life skill; it's a crucial one. Peer pressure can manifest in various ways, both subtle and overt, and the ability to navigate it effectively can make all the difference in maintaining one's integrity and well-being.

Understanding the dynamics of peer pressure is the first step toward resilience. Peer pressure can take the form of direct instructions or more subtle hints. It can be positive, encouraging individuals to engage in healthy behaviors, or negative, pushing them toward potentially harmful actions. Recognizing these nuances is vital for developing strategies to combat them.

One of the most powerful defenses against peer pressure is a strong sense of self. It starts with knowing who you are, understanding your values, and recognizing your limits. When you have a clear grasp of your identity and beliefs, it becomes easier to make decisions that align with your principles, even when confronted with pressure to do otherwise. Confidence in your values acts as a shield against external influence.

Assertiveness is another critical skill in resisting peer pressure. Being assertive means confidently expressing your thoughts and feelings without being passive or aggressive. It allows you to firmly stand up for yourself and your beliefs while maintaining respect for others. When you can assertively communicate your boundaries, you become less susceptible to external pressures.

Supportive relationships play a pivotal role in resisting peer pressure. Surrounding yourself with friends and family who respect your choices and encourage you to stay true to your values provides a robust defense. These positive connections serve as a buffer against negative peer influences. Spending time with people who support your autonomy and values can help you stay resolute in your decisions.

Learning to say "no" assertively is a cornerstone of peer pressure resistance. Practicing how to decline unwanted requests or suggestions with confidence is crucial. Saying "no" doesn't have to be confrontational; it can be done calmly and politely, yet firmly. When you can assertively refuse to participate in something against your values, you take control of the situation.

Planning ahead for situations where you might face peer pressure is another effective strategy. Anticipate scenarios where you could encounter pressure and prepare your responses in advance. This might involve avoiding specific environments, having an exit strategy, or identifying a trusted person you can reach out to for support.

Finally, it's essential to consider the consequences of your actions. Reflect on how giving in to peer pressure might impact your life in both the short term and the long run. This reflective exercise can help you prioritize what truly matters and make choices that align with your values and well-being.

In conclusion, dealing with peer pressure is a skill that empowers individuals to maintain their integrity and make choices in their best interest. Understanding the complexities of peer pressure, bolstering self-confidence, cultivating assertiveness, nurturing supportive relationships, mastering the art of saying "no," planning for challenging situations, and contemplating consequences are all valuable tools in the toolkit for effectively navigating the pressures of social influence.

Saying No

To deal with peer pressure, you need to be able to say "no," which is an easy but sometimes tough thing to do. Knowing how to say "no" is essential, especially when something goes against your morals, beliefs, or comfort is paramount. Assertive refusal isn't just a way to stay away from bad people; it's also a way to stay true to yourself and make decisions that are best for you.

Be honest and strong when you say "no." This works well for many people. This doesn't mean being mean or rude, but it does mean being honest and clear. Telling someone at a party, "No, thank you, I don't drink," is an excellent and clear way to say no to a drink. There's no need for long reasons or explanations. Don't forget that you have the freedom to make decisions that align with your views and comfort level.

One more thing you can do is offer an option. If you feel like you have to do something you don't want to, suggesting a related but different action can help you get what you want. If your friends want to go to a party late at night and you're not interested, you could suggest a day trip or a movie night at your house instead. Giving them an option shows that you still want to hang out with your friends, but in a way that works better for you.

It can also help to think about what you'll say ahead of time, especially if you know you'll be in a setting where you might have to deal with peer pressure. Think about the different situations you could face and how you would like to handle them. If you have a plan ready, it can be easier to say no at the last minute.

Having faith in yourself is also essential. Sticking to your choices is easier when you have faith in yourself and your choices. Self-confidence takes time, but the first step is believing you can choose what's best for you.

Taking yourself out of a situation is sometimes the best thing you can do. If you're constantly being pushed to do things you don't want to, you might want to think about whether these are the people you want to spend time with. Spending time with people who accept your choices and boundaries can make it a lot less likely that you have to say "no."

Finally, one important part of saying no is realizing that letting people down is okay. There are people you can't please, and that's okay. Your first duty is to take care of yourself and your health. People who care about you will accept your choices, even if they don't agree or fully understand them.

Basically, being able to say "no" is a very important skill for staying honest and independent. Being direct, giving alternatives, planning responses, boosting your confidence, staying away from bad situations, and realizing it's okay to let people down are all parts of it. You can make valid decisions about who you are and what you believe in when you learn how to say "no."

Boundaries and Respect

Setting boundaries is important for keeping a good relationship, whether it's with friends, family, or a romantic partner. We set boundaries, or imaginary lines, around how we want to be treated and what we're okay with or not okay with. They are necessary for people to accept and understand each other. It is important to respect others and our limits to build trust and ensure that everyone feels safe and valued.

Being aware of yourself is the first step in setting limits. You must know your beliefs, limits, and comfort zones to do this. One example is that you might be okay with people borrowing books but not money. You may also enjoy being with other people but need time to yourself to recover. The first step in setting boundaries is to be aware of these unique preferences.

It's just as important to be clear and polite about your limits. If you know your limits, you need to be able to tell other people what they are. It can be scary to be honest with people, especially if you're worried about how they will respond. But being honest is important for healthy relationships. Do not lose your cool when you set limits. Be calm and firm. It's not about giving threats or requests; it's about being clear about what you need in a way that is kind to yourself and others.

Along with setting your own limits, respecting those others have set is important. Listen to what someone says about what makes them feel good and what makes them feel bad, and then respect that. You need to know that everyone has their own comfort zone and limits, and what's fine for one person might not be fine for someone else. When you respect their limits, you show that you care about the other person's feelings and needs.

Boundaries can be very different for each person, including everything from time and energy to physical room and things. They can also change over time, so it's good to talk about what does and doesn't work in a relationship all the time.

Another thing that's important to remember is that setting and following rules goes both ways. It requires giving in and negotiating. If you want to keep the relationship going, you may need to change your limits sometimes. Other times, you may need to be strict. To keep your own sense of self, you need to find a balance that takes everyone's needs into account.

Finally, it's important to know that setting limits doesn't make you rude or selfish. It helps you understand how valuable you are and treat yourself with care. People who really care about you will accept your limits and value your honesty.

To sum up, good relationships are built on respect and setting limits. They include being aware of and clear about your own limits, accepting the limits of others, and being willing to talk and find a middle ground. Setting and standing by limits builds trust and respect, which is essential for relationships to grow.

I remember the first time I learned how important it is to set limits and treat others respectfully. It was my second year of high school, and my friendships were the most important thing in my life at that time.

I couldn't live without my friend Luke. It felt like the best relationship ever because we told each other everything, from secrets to homework. As Luke asked for more and more of my time, things began to change. It began with small requests, like meeting up every day after school. Soon, though, he wanted to hang out with me every weekend, too. That left me with no time for other people or even myself.

I didn't mind at first. In the end, Luke was my best friend. But as time went on, I felt like I couldn't handle everything. I had other friends I wanted to see and things I liked to do, and sometimes I just needed some alone time. I was afraid to tell Luke this, though. That would have made him feel bad or like I didn't value our friendship.

Luke asked me to ride a bike one weekend, but I was already booked with another friend. He got mad when I told him this and said I wasn't paying attention to our friendship. When I saw that, I realized how fuzzy our lines had become. I let Luke decide how I spent my time, and I forgot about my own needs and other people I was close to.

I thought about our friendship as I lay in bed that night. I saw that I hadn't made my rules clear for Luke. I hadn't told them that I needed time and room for other relationships. I tried to avoid these talks to keep the peace, but they made things worse.

I chose to have a serious conversation with Luke the next day. When we met at our favorite coffee shop, I told him how much I appreciated our friendship. Then, I told them in a gentle way that my life needed more balance. I told them how I felt about needing time with other people, hobbies, and time to be alone. I told him that this didn't change how much I valued our relationship.

Luke seemed to understand, which surprised me. His own admission was that he had been worried about losing our company, which is why he had been holding on so tight. As a friend, we decided to make our rules more clear. We agreed it was fine to spend time apart, do different things, and hang out with other people. Not only did this talk make our friendship stronger, it also made me feel freer and more appreciated.

This taught me a fundamental lesson about how important it is to respect each other and set limits in any relationship. It showed me that being honest with someone can make your relationship better and more satisfying, even if it's hard. It also taught me how important it is to take care of my own needs, which I had forgotten to do because I wanted to be a good friend.

After that, I made it a point to be clearer about my limits in all of my relationships. I learned that limits aren't things that get in the way; they're the rules that make relationships grow and thrive. Finally, I learned that a real friend will always honor your limits and value your honesty.

In the final chapter, we'll wrap up our journey with a recap of the key life skills.

Chapter 9: Bringing It All Together

As we start this final chapter, it's time to think about the journey we've been on and all the skills, insights, and experiences we've gained. This chapter is like being on a high ground and looking back at the road we've been on. Then, we turn around to face the bright future that lies ahead. We want to discuss how all our lessons can be put together to help us grow and succeed.

Your Path to a Bright Future

Picture reading these chapters as a hike up a mountain. Every step, no matter how big or small, has taught you something new and helped you become stronger. Now that we've reached the top, we can take a moment to breathe, look out over the wide view, and remember the bright future that your new skills and knowledge can help you make.

You've learned about many aspects of personal growth along the way, such as how to set and reach goals, understand emotional intelligence, deal with peer pressure, and build healthy relationships. Each part was like adding a new tool to your collection; it helped you get ready for the varied and often unpredictable journey that life will be.

Developing a Personal Action Plan

Making a personal action plan is an important part of turning all the lessons and skills you've learned into something you can use. You should use the ideas you learn in each chapter as a guide for your personal and professional growth. You could think of it as making a plan for your future that fits your beliefs, goals, and aspirations.

Setting clear, attainable goals is the first thing you should do when making your own action plan. What you've learned about yourself and what you want to achieve should show up in these goals. They could be anything from raising your emotional intelligence, strengthening your relationships, and achieving specific academic or job goals. Making sure your goals are Specific, Measurable, Achievable, Relevant, and Time-bound is easy if you use the SMART method.

Next, think about what skills and tools you already have and what you might need to reach your goals. This could mean getting more education, training, a guide, or even just practicing in certain areas more. Figure out what skills or information you don't have enough of and make a plan for how you will get them. This could mean taking classes, looking for teachers, or setting aside time to study on your own.

Managing your time is an important part of your action plan. Break your big goals down into smaller, more manageable jobs, and give each one a due date. This breaks down the jobs into smaller pieces that are easier to handle and helps you track your progress. Set aside specific times in your calendar to do these things. This will help you stay on track with your goals.

Your personal action plan should also include ways to get around any problems that might come up. Think about the things that might hinder you from reaching your goals and plan how you will deal with them. Creating ways to deal with worry, making a support system, or making plans for what to do if things don't go as planned could be part of this.

Your action plan also includes essential parts for reflection and change. Check-in on your progress toward your goals often, and be ready to make changes as needed. Life is hard to plan for, and your wants and goals may change over time. An action plan that works is fluid and can change as your situation and knowledge grow.

Finally, you should include self-care in your action plan. Your health and well-being shouldn't suffer in order to reach your goals. Make sure your plan includes time to unwind, do fun things, and connect with family and friends. For long-term success and personal happiness, balance is very important.

Seeking Mentorship and Guidance

Seeking mentorship is a crucial aspect of personal and professional development, akin to having a guiding light to navigate the complexities of life's journey. Mentors offer invaluable insights, wisdom, and fresh perspectives based on their experiences and knowledge. They serve as beacons, helping individuals navigate through challenges, sparking innovative ideas, and fostering personal growth. In an ever-evolving world, having a mentor can provide much-needed clarity and guidance.

To embark on the journey of finding the right mentor, it is essential to first identify the areas in which one seeks assistance. Whether it's advancing in a career, nurturing personal growth, excelling in academics, or acquiring specific skills, clarity about one's needs is paramount. Once these needs are well-defined, the search for individuals who have achieved the success or knowledge sought can begin. Mentors can be found among experts in the desired field, teachers, family members, or community leaders. It's worth noting that mentors need not always be luminaries; those a few steps ahead on a similar path can be equally impactful guides.

When approaching someone to be a mentor, it is vital to articulate the reasons for seeking their guidance and why they were chosen for this role. Most individuals are receptive to mentorship requests and are willing to share their knowledge. However, clarity about expectations and the specific areas in which mentorship is desired can make the interaction more meaningful and productive.

Mentorship takes on various forms, from formal agreements with defined schedules to informal arrangements such as regular coffee meetings. Some mentorships span years, while others are geared towards addressing specific challenges or goals. Regardless of the structure, mentorship is a dynamic relationship that fosters growth, learning, and personal development.

In summary, finding a mentor and seeking their guidance is an invaluable endeavor for personal and professional growth. Mentors offer advice, support, and encouragement that are instrumental in navigating life's complexities and achieving goals. Through active engagement in mentorship relationships, individuals can gain knowledge and experiences that may be otherwise challenging to acquire independently. A commitment to learning and improvement, coupled with an open mind, is the key to maximizing the benefits of mentorship.

Inspiration

Mark Zuckerberg went from being a computer-crazy teenager to becoming one of the most important tech leaders. His story is both inspiring and enlightening. Mark was born on May 14, 1984, in White Plains, New York. He became interested and good at programming at a young age. This interest grew in a home that encouraged it; his dad even hired a software developer to teach him on the side. Putting money into his skills early on setting the stage for what was to come.

Mark was not only a great student in high school, but he also loved programming. He used his skills to make a number of programs, such as Synapse, a music player, and a communication tool for his father's dentist's office. One exciting thing about Synapse was that it used AI to learn how the user usually listened to music, which was new at the time. Lots of big companies, like AOL and Microsoft, were interested in this project because they saw how talented this young worker was. Even though these tech giants offered Mark jobs, he chose to continue his education. This showed how much he wanted to improve his skills and knowledge.

Mark began the process of making Facebook at Harvard University. At first, he made a tool called CourseMatch that let students pick classes by looking at what other users had chosen. Then, he made Facemash, a website where students could rate how attractive each other was. Even though they were controversial, these projects set the stage for his biggest project yet.

In 2004, Mark started "Thefacebook," which was first meant to be a social networking site for Harvard students. It was a simple but powerful idea to make a place where students could quickly share information and connect with each other. The website became very famous quickly, spreading to other Ivy League schools and colleges all over the country.

Facebook's rapid growth made it hard to keep up with everything. Mark had to manage his schoolwork at Harvard and the growth of an online site at the same time. Other students sued Mark because they thought he stole their idea for the website because it was so popular. The young businessman, who was still in his teens, was going through some tough times.

Still, Mark never wavered in his faith in his plan for Facebook. He was incredibly tough and flexible, which would shape the way he did business and came up with new ideas. In the summer of 2004, he went to Silicon Valley. By the end of that year, a million people had joined Facebook. This was the start of something that would spread around the world.

The story of Mark Zuckerberg shows how powerful emotion, vision, and toughness can be. As a kid, he didn't just wish to be successful; he worked hard and was determined to get there. His story gives hope to people who want to be businesses and anyone else with a dream and the guts to go after it. It shows that anyone of any age can do amazing things if they have the right mix of ability, hard work, and a willingness to learn and change.

Final Words

I want to send sincere congratulations and best wishes for the future to all the amazing teens who have been with me through all these chapters. You've come a long way in learning about essential things in life.

Remember, the path you're walking now is unique and full of possibilities. You have the potential to shape not just your future but the world around you. Stay curious, keep an open mind, and never be afraid to ask for help or seek guidance when you need it. Remember that success is not just about reaching a destination but about the journey and the person you become along the way.

You have the strength, the intelligence, and the creativity to make a positive impact in your world. Believe in yourself and your abilities. Be kind to yourself and others, and never underestimate the power of empathy and understanding.

"Many of life's failures are people who did not realize how close they were to success when they gave up."

Thomas A. Edison

Références

15 Tips to Build Self Esteem and Confidence in Teens. (n.d.). Big Life Journal. https://biglifejournal.com/blogs/blog/build-self-esteem-confidence-teens

How to Build Self-Esteem in Children and Teens. (2022, May 16). Healthcare Network. https://healthcareswfl.org/how-to-build-self-esteem-in-children-and-teens/

Shier, M. (2020, September 11). *6.1 Test Anxiety and How to Manage It*. Pressbooks. https://opentextbc.ca/studentsuccess/chapter/test-anxiety/

Shier, M. (2020, September 11). *6.1 Test Anxiety and How to Manage It*. Pressbooks. https://opentextbc.ca/studentsuccess/chapter/test-anxiety

Aqeel, N. (2023, November 22). *Financial Literacy Among Teens & Tweens - Neelum Aqeel - Medium*. Medium. https://medium.com/@neelumaqeel/financial-literacy-among-teens-tweens-37a53f8349c7

S. (2023, July 14). *Empowering Teens: A Guide to Earning Money and Building Financial Independence*. Medium. https://medium.com/@pawelwoj2009/empowering-teens-a-guide-to-earning-money-and-building-financial-independence-6fba2da69abc

Financial Literacy for Teens and Students. (n.d.). PPT. https://www.slideshare.net/Experian_US/financial-literacy-for-teens-and-students

Decision Making/Problem Solving With Teens. (n.d.). Ohioline. https://ohioline.osu.edu/factsheet/HYG-5301

Problem-solving steps: pre-teens and teenagers. (2021, November 5). Raising Children Network. https://raisingchildren.net.au/pre-teens/behaviour/encouraging-good-behaviour/problem-solving-steps

Dray, J. (2021, July 8). *Child and Adolescent Mental Health and Resilience-Focussed Interventions: A Conceptual Analysis to Inform Future Research*. International Journal of Environmental Research and Public Health. https://doi.org/10.3390/ijerph18147315

nonverbal communication skills: Topics by Science.gov. (n.d.). https://www.science.gov/topicpages/n/nonverbal+communication+skills.html

Relationship Communication Skills For Teenagers. (n.d.). Planned Parenthood. https://www.plannedparenthood.org/learn/teens/relationships/all-about-communication

Early Is Better: 15 Effective Communication Skills For Kids And Teenagers. (2023, August 8). Everand. https://www.everand.com/book/663968641/Early-Is-Better-15-Effective-Communication-Skills-For-Kids-And-Teenagers

Jhangiani, R. (2022, January 26). *3.2 The Feeling Self: Self-Esteem*. Pressbooks. https://opentextbc.ca/socialpsychology/chapter/the-feeling-self-self-esteem/

Ampel, B. M. P. A. C. (2020, November 2). *The Self Confidence Workbook: A Guide to Overcoming Self-Doubt and Improving Self-Esteem*. ICRRD Journal. https://icrrd.com/article/143/the-self-confidence-workbook-a-guide-to-overcoming-self-doubt-and-improving-self-esteem

Ampel, B. M. P. A. C. (2020, November 2). *The Self Confidence Workbook: A Guide to Overcoming Self-Doubt and Improving Self-Esteem*. ICRRD Journal. https://icrrd.com/article/143/the-self-confidence-workbook-a-guide-to-overcoming-self-doubt-and-improving-self-esteem

Cairns, A., Kavanagh, D. J., Dark, F., & McPhail, S. (2019, July 9). *Goal setting improves retention in youth mental health: a cross-sectional analysis*. Child and Adolescent Psychiatry and Mental Health. https://doi.org/10.1186/s13034-019-0288-x

MSc, L. W. B. (2022, August 22). *7.1 Emotions and Intelligence*. Pressbooks. https://ecampusontario.pressbooks.pub/conflictmanagement/chapter/7-1-emotions-and-intelligence/

Hoose, N. A. V. (n.d.). *Peer Relationships | Adolescent Psychology*. https://courses.lumenlearning.com/adolescent/chapter/peer-relationships/

16 Examples of Mentorship Goals for Your Organization | Together Mentoring Software. (n.d.). https://www.togetherplatform.com/blog/examples-of-mentoring-program-goals

www.ingramcontent.com/pod-product-compliance
Lightning Source LLC
Chambersburg PA
CBHW052145070526
44585CB00017B/1985